You in Your Small Corner

A testimony of how an extraordinary
God intervened in the life of a very
ordinary housewife.

Elizabeth Loynes

O&U
Onwards & Upwards

Onwards and Upwards Publishers

4 The Old Smithy
London Road
Rockbeare
EX5 2EA
United Kingdom
www.onwardsandupwards.org

First edition, published in the United Kingdom by Onwards and Upwards Publishers Ltd. (2021).

ISBN: 978-1-78815-906-7
Typeface: Sabon LT

Author's Note:

I have tried to recreate events, locales and conversations from my memories of them. In order to protect their privacy, in some places I have changed the names of individuals and identifying characteristics such as physical properties, occupations and the names of places.

Endorsements

This autobiography is the story of a woman devoted to the love and care of her family, who through all the trials and difficulties of her life finds strength in her Christian faith. Gently inspiring and uplifting.

Wendy Craig

It has been a pleasure to read, and now to commend, *You in Your Small Corner.* This is Elizabeth's life story, which ... is well written with a refreshing honesty and an inspiring reality. Elizabeth shares the challenges of her early life, the joy of marriage and babies, growing cold in her faith and meeting God again, the grief of losing close friends, the pain of divorce, the surprise of remarriage, the challenge of her husband's depression and opportunities for Christian service. Yet through it all, God's grace shines through ... In a world full of celebrities and big headlines, this is the story of the King of the Universe working in one small corner of the world, away from the blaze of publicity! And He can work in your corner too!

Revd Nicolas R.S. Lowe BSc, PhD

About the Author

 Elizabeth is married with three daughters and five grandchildren. Most of her paid working career was as an administrator / PA / secretary. As part of her service in the church, Elizabeth was involved in singing and leading worship, prayer ministry and counselling. She and her husband ran a church house group and later a group for seniors, and she also helped with a church coffee shop which provided community lunches. Her personal hobbies include painting with watercolours and acrylics, sewing, reading and playing bridge.

To contact Elizabeth, please write to:

Elizabeth Loynes
c/o Onwards and Upwards Publishers,
4 The Old Smithy, London Road,
Rockbeare, EX5 7DX

Or send an email to:

elizabethrloynes@hotmail.com

Or visit the book's webpage for more information:

www.onwardsandupwards.org/**you-in-your-small-corner**

Contents

You in Your Small Corner

Jesus bids us shine,
With a pure, clear light,
Like a little candle,
Burning in the night.
In this world is darkness,
We must shine –
You in your small corner,
And I in mine.

Jesus bids us shine,
First of all for Him;
Well He sees and knows it,
If our light grows dim;
He looks down from heaven,
To see us shine –
You in your small corner,
And I in mine.

Jesus bids us shine,
Then, for all around
Many kinds of darkness
In this world are found –
Sin, and want, and sorrow;
So we must shine,
You in your small corner,
And I in mine.

Susan Bogert Warner
1819-1885

You in Your Small Corner

Preface

IT IS MAY 2020 – WE HAVE BEEN IN LOCKDOWN SINCE 23 March. I believe God has given me the task of recording my thoughts and testimony:

> *I remember the days of long ago; I meditate on all your works and consider what your hands have done.*[1]

Coronavirus lockdown has certainly given me more time to reflect on what God has done over the years. I received a confirmation of what I was sensing from God from my granddaughter in Germany, who suggested I might write about my life and experiences.

Long before the lockdown, my husband and I had booked a two-week holiday in Portugal in March. The coronavirus in the U.K. had begun towards the end of January, imported from abroad, and was gradually increasing and taking hold. We had not been advised officially against travel and so the holiday went ahead. I was not worried about Portugal, where the infection rates were far less than in the U.K., but I was very nervous about being in Gatwick Airport and flying. Feeling very anxious, I sent up a silent prayer in panic as we were entering Gatwick Airport, and Jesus spoke into my ear so clearly – almost audibly – "I am here." How that filled my heart with joy and what a difference that made! I was able to cope with the airport and all that entailed with great confidence and assurance. *Thank You, Lord, for your promise that you are always with me and thank You for that special occasion so recently when I knew You were there with me in no uncertain terms.*

This story is about how Jesus has been there in every circumstance of my life and has guided each step of the way. My aim is to give glory to Him, and also my prayer is that you will see God's hand at work in your own life and respond to Him with renewed faith and service.

---

[1] Psalm 143:5

You in Your Small Corner

Foreword

GOD GIVES US TIMES OF GLADNESS AND TIMES OF SADNESS. Consequently we are never guaranteed lives which are free from suffering. Quite the contrary! But is there any valid reason why some people suffer much more than others? This is a difficult question that every generation in human history has had to face. Whose fault is it when bad things happen? Where is God in my time of need?

The author of *You in Your Small Corner* experienced many great challenges. She asked, 'Dear Lord, why have You allowed this to happen?' But she also knew, like Job of old, that God was with her. For these reasons, it was a delight to my heart and soul to read this remarkable story about how God intervened in the life of a very ordinary housewife. She can look back and reflect on God's faithfulness in every crisis of life. Furthermore, she knows that the best is yet to come for those who accept the promises of God.

Although it is a short book, it is not short on sound advice in dealing with the problems of family life. I was certainly encouraged by the strong biblical convictions of the author and it will, I guarantee, provide practical and spiritual encouragement in the midst of difficulties. I commend this work wholeheartedly to the reader.

Christopher Brearley
Former elder
St John's Wood Road Baptist Church, London

You in Your Small Corner

CHAPTER ONE

The Beginning

IT WAS EASY TO DECIDE HOW COLD THE DAY WAS OUTSIDE – when I awoke, there would be ice patterns on the window. If the ice covered halfway up, then that was normal – if the ice covered nearly all the window, then it was very cold. I drew the clothes lying by the side of the bed where I had taken them off, slipped them into the bed and warmed them the best I could.

I would dress – at least my undergarments and socks – while still inside the bedclothes. It was so cold in the bedroom, you had to have some clothes on before getting out of bed. We didn't have rubber hot water bottles, and electric blankets were not yet invented. We had a hard stone hot water bottle which both scalded you and burnt your flesh on getting into bed and later became an ice cold lump in the bed by the next morning. God bless whoever invented rubber hot water bottles!

Getting dressed was at top speed, and within a very few minutes I was dressed and downstairs looking for breakfast. There was no inside bathroom, and a hasty wash, commonly called a 'cat's lick and a promise', was in the kitchen sink with cold water. Kettles had to be boiled if we wanted hot water so a quick splash over my face sufficed. Another top speed exercise was going out to the outside loo!

How glad I was that I never needed the loo in the night-time; there was no light out there, and if you wanted to go after dark, the only option was a candle (which sometimes blew out if it was windy). In the dim light I imagined spiders and all sorts of creepy crawlies, hence no visits after dusk. The phobia about spiders and creepy crawlies has stayed with me. My husband laughs as any programmes on TV showing such creatures make my flesh creep and my scalp itch. It is incredible how many nature programmes all seem to contain a myriad of ants and spiders!

Mum and Dad had a pot under their bed, but I was determined to manage without it until the morning. 'Mod cons' were not heard of. Loo roll consisted of bits of newspaper threaded onto a string. There was only one electric light in each room and, as I said, no hot water. In the early years Mum used to have two black flat irons with which she used to do the ironing, on a blanket on the table. One would heat up by being close to the coal fire whilst the other was used for ironing. As that one cooled, she would swap it for the other one. Later on she was happy to get the new innovation: an electric iron! No such thing as steam though; a piece of rag or old hankie wetted with water sufficed. A great idea was to take an old salad cream bottle and make small holes in the lid so that when it was filled with water you could use it as a shaker and shake droplets of water over the clothes.

It was a lengthy event to wash my hair. The bowl in the sink had some warmed water in it, and I would use soap, or later on some new revolutionary soap flakes, to wash my hair. Mum would then pour jugs of water over my head to wash away the soap. My hair was long and often got tangled, and one of the best inventions ever as far as I was concerned was the new cream rinse – a prelude to modern day conditioners. To have something to rid me of tangles was a marvel. Before cream rinse was invented, I can remember sitting on the living room table whilst Dad combed the tangles out of my hair. "If you can keep from crying, I can keep you from laughing," he used to say every time as he pulled and pulled on my hair to get the comb through.

Bath time was once a week, and the tin bath that lived on the wall outside was brought indoors, placed in front of the fire and filled with hot water heated in the kettle or saucepans on the gas stove. We all took turns to bathe in the same bath-full of water; luckily, I was first as I was the youngest. Sometimes, however, I was not able to bath at all, and this was due to my eczema.

It was a mystery where my eczema came from as it is supposed to be hereditary, yet I was the first one in the family to have it. Indeed, in searching for a reason for my eczema, the doctors thought that maybe my mother lacked proper nourishment and vitamins because of the war years and that may have contributed to the condition. I know also that eczema is a nervous complaint and affected by a person's wellbeing, and since my mother was a person easily worried and anxious, I wonder if that contributed as well. Nowadays it seems that more and more people are affected by eczema, asthma and hay fever, but then it was rare.

I cannot remember a time when I was free of eczema and I must have had this condition from a very young age. At times, when my skin was bad, it would itch constantly and there would be weeping sores, and at those times I did not have a bath because my mother used to cleanse my skin using olive oil. Soap and water only made it worse.

I was often bandaged from my fingertips to past my elbows, and when the bandages came off, layers of skin came off too. At bedtime Mum would remove my bandages and gently rub my skin with the olive oil to clean it. Then clean washed bandages would be applied, and I would see the rug on the floor literally covered with flakes of my skin. Bandages were expensive, so each bandage would be washed, ironed and reused several times until they became too frayed to use again. I became adept at bandaging myself using one hand and my teeth to tie the knots.

There was no medication then, and the only thing the doctor suggested was that my mother used splints to prevent my scratching. As it was, I wore cotton gloves to bed so that I would not do too much damage scratching in my sleep. As I got older, my mother paid for me to see a skin specialist, and it cost her a lot of money they could ill afford. That lady was kind and suggested dusting my skin with a brownish powder that contained I knew not what. She also used electrotherapy, and I used to sit with electrodes on either arm whilst a current was passed through. Whether that did any good, I don't know. My other treatment which would horrify doctors today was to stand near naked in front of ultraviolet lamps so my skin could absorb UV rays. Obviously in those days no one was worried about skin cancer! The general opinion was that things would improve in my teens, which they did to a degree, but I will always remember going to school with bandages from fingertip to armpit.

Breakfast was in the living room, one main room where the family ate and did everything. There was a coal fire and a wireless set in the corner. I can remember the very auspicious day when we exchanged our old wireless for a new radio. We used to listen to *The Archers,* and I especially liked a serial called *Tales of Outer Space* and 'Lemme' the adventurer who always seemed to get into danger just at the end of the episode, so that you would have to listen in next week to find out what happened to him. We didn't have cereal for breakfast – that only came later. Eggs or toast was the order of the day, along with tea of course. We had no refrigerator so any milk left from the day before had been boiled in order to keep it from going sour overnight. How I hated tea in the morning using boiled milk; it had bits floating on the top, and try as I might, I never could manage to fish them all out.

In the early days I had a lift to infant school on the back of my mum's bicycle. On moving into junior school, I was deemed old enough to walk there on my own. School was awful; my eczema was not a pretty sight, and I found myself an outcast as other children would not come anywhere near me for fear of catching it. There was a lovely red-haired teacher called Miss Missit who helped the best she could. She lifted me up and held me in her arms. "There," she said, "I am not catching it." One girl called Patricia was a particularly unpleasant bully. She and her group of 'friends' would wait for me outside the school gate. The only bit of school I enjoyed was art, and my pride and joy was a painting I did of Hiawatha. Even doing P.E. was hazardous. We used the main hall and had to balance by walking on the underside of the long forms used for assembly. These forms linked together with metal hooks on the end, and one day I fell and cut my chin open. That meant a visit to the City Infirmary for stitches.

Another hospital visit was because I lost the tip of my right index finger. If the front door was open, plus the door from the hall into the living room, the door from the living room into the kitchen and finally the back door into the yard, a strong wind could occasionally rush through the house. It was on one such occasion that I was standing by the front door which slammed shut, catching one of my fingers of my right hand and chopping the end off. I had been for some treatment for my eczema and my legs were stiff, and I couldn't move quickly enough to avoid the door. Dad took me to the infirmary, and they asked him if he had brought the bit of finger as they could have sewed it back on. However, he had not, so to this day my right index finger is shorter than my left one. It was difficult to use the finger for a while, but playing piano, and later on learning touch typing, enabled me to use it fully again.

Most of my younger years were quite lonely. We had a spare bedroom at the back of the house and this room was completely empty of any furniture. It was totally bare except for my assortment of dolls and teddies which I used to sit in a circle for company. My mother was in her mid-forties when I was born, and my father was not pleased to have another girl. They had had a son prior to me but, sadly, he died whilst still a baby, and so when I was born, I was named Rosemary for remembrance of my dead brother and Elizabeth after my mum. My eldest sister was much older than me; Phyllis was married to Ken at the end of the war and I was her bridesmaid at the age of three. Parents love to remind their children of any *faux pas*, and I was told that during the ceremony my small shrill voice was heard piping up loudly, "My flowers are dying." Phyllis used to take me out for walks sometimes and people assumed that I was her daughter instead of her younger sister. Family planning was not a strong point, and my other older sister Beryl was eleven years older than me. Consequently, when she was in her teens and wanting to date her boyfriend, I was a nuisance and always in the way. I don't know how old my older brother would have been; all I knew was that the local C of E church were not able to bury him in consecrated ground because he had not been christened. Obviously, that was very upsetting for my mum and that was the reason she started to attend New Road Baptist Church.

Born in 1943, my earliest memories are from after the end of the war. Things were still very scarce, and there was food rationing and rationing for all sorts of things that went on for years. I used to go shopping to the local shops with my mum. Near the railway station was a greengrocers we used frequently, and there was a corner shop just opposite our house. There was a Co-op in George Street where mum shopped and it was quite large with counters on three sides. (There were no supermarkets until many years later.) As you paid for items at each counter, the money was put into a small conical metal container and this went zooming across the ceiling on a pulley to the cash desk, which was high up in one corner. Any change was returned in the same way, again using the container on a pulley. Mum collected her "divi" (short for dividends) once a year, and it was a means of treats by way of celebration.

My mum had to save up for everything, as Dad only gave her a fixed sum for housekeeping. She saved for years to buy small comforts like a new clock or a carpet for the front room. The front room was a parlour containing the best furniture and a piano. This room was only used and had a fire lit at Christmas or for special visitors, of which, as far as I knew, there were none.

On a Saturday morning we would make our usual visit to the covered market in the Cornmarket Street. This was where Mum would buy our Sunday joint of meat, plus some fresh fish for our Saturday meal. Dad came from Cromer in Norfolk and was very fond of herrings as he had virtually been brought up on the local fish. Today there is an interesting museum near Great Yarmouth that tells the story of the girls who travelled down south following the fishing boats and gutting the herring and salting them. Cromer crab and herring were a favourite meal for us too.

Going back to the Sunday joint of meat, this of course used to last Sunday, Monday and sometimes even Tuesday. On Monday we would eat the cold meat and on Tuesdays rissoles, which today would be similar to a burger made from the minced-up meat. Monday was washing day and this was a great marathon of a task. First, water had to be bucketed from the tap to the copper in the corner and a fire lit under it to heat the water. The mangle was brought in from the back yard along with the tin bath to catch the expressed water. Washing was boiled in the copper and rinsed in the sink in cold water. There was an old-fashioned scrubbing board and scrubbing brush and a bar of hard soap. I sometimes used to turn the handle for the mangle and other times catch the stiffened sheets as they came through the mangle out the other side. Washing took all day on Monday, hence the reason for cold meat for our meal.

One particular washing day it was very hot and my hair was bothering me, so I asked mum to tie it up. She was too busy to stop what she was doing and so ignored my request, so I cut some of my long hair with scissors. Of course, that caused a rumpus, and I then had to go to the hairdresser to get it cut properly!

I should tell you a little about my father who, as I said, was born in Cromer. He was an only child, and throughout my childhood I learned very little about my paternal grandparents. However, I found out later that he did have an adopted/fostered sibling and for some reason fell out with the family and left home and never went back. I never met Grandmother, but Mum and Dad must have lived near them at some point because Mum spoke of how she was criticised if the pots and pans were not gleaming and shining. Dad lied about his age and joined the Navy in the First World War. He was on a destroyer in Scapa Flow near the north of Scotland. I found it amazing he was in the navy considering that he never learned to swim, but the waters where they sailed were so cold you would have died pretty quickly anyway, swimmer or not. I have inherited his 'diddy box', which has been made into a sewing box. This lovely polished wooden box used to contain all a sailor's personal items and bears the initials of my grandfather as well as my father.

At one time Dad owned his own baker's shop but when the "new sliced bread" was invented, the shop went out of business. He had various jobs, and times were hard for everyone during the thirties' depression. Eventually he came to Oxford looking for work. He began working in the bakery in St Thomas Street, Oxford, and the house we lived in was a house tied to his job. He was not required to sign up in the Second World War because he was a baker and that was a reserved occupation. Bakers' hours are unsocial, and he worked through the night baking bread for the next day. He was also a confectioner – recipes then used dried egg because real eggs were scarce. He did, however, make real chocolate Easter eggs and decorated them with sugar flowers. Easter eggs used to be made by coating a metal mould with chocolate, letting it set and then adding further layers to gradually build up the thickness of chocolate until the egg was strong enough to be put together and decorated. Years later I used to try to make royal icing and decorate Christmas and other cakes but probably never to his standard, although I was not allowed to see any of his work. Because of the night shift, I had to be quiet about the house and he usually got up around four o'clock in the afternoon.

Dad was uncommunicative, and the only times we had happy days together were on holiday, although he did occasionally accompany me so that I could ride my bike around Port Meadow. Once a year we would vary our bicycle ride to St Giles to see the fair people erecting the annual fair. St Giles, a large tree-lined main road, was closed to traffic every year for the fair to be held on the first Monday and Tuesday, following the first Sunday in September. This was an annual highlight and not to be missed. Many years later I was thrilled to take my own children and grandchildren to the fair, which has hardly changed over the years except for the addition of some large modern rides. The usual trappings accompanied a visit to the fair – candy floss, a helium balloon and a 'fairy' doll. In a life with very few outings and treats, the fair was a yearly delight.

In modern Oxford there is no sign left of the Oxpens, where I used to visit regularly as a child looking at all the animals at the cattle market. The whole area has been redeveloped, much of the original housing probably designated for improvement. The house I lived in opened straight onto the street which served as a playground for skipping and Queenie and other games, as there were few gardens and the only green space some distance away. Of course, the traffic then was minimal. The corner shop just across the road used to sell items wrapped in blue paper and an occasional treat was an ice cream. This came in the form of a circular blue paper tube containing the ice cream, which was sliced and placed in a cornet. When we had no fridge, let alone a freezer, an ice cream was delicious.

On holiday Dad was a different person. We lived very simply with, as I said before, no 'mod cons' – no TV, no car, no phone, just one visit to a 'panto' at Christmas where we got the cheapest seats up in the gods. The New Theatre at Oxford is largely unchanged and still provides avid memories of the treat that was the pantomime. The annual holiday time was always the two weeks at the beginning of the school summer break, these weeks being the regular pattern of the Cowley factory shutdown. We felt highly privileged to get a week at the seaside, and this was a special treat a lot of other families did not get. We went to Clacton on Sea each year and took the train to London Paddington. From there we went on the underground to Liverpool Street station and from there caught the train to Clacton. The trains were always crowded, and you were very lucky if you got a seat. Most of the time I used to sit on the suitcase. We had one very large suitcase, and I never used to think anything of it as my dad carried it. Today we have suitcases on wheels, but then it must have been a very heavy thing to lift. At Liverpool Street station there were long queues of people waiting for the Clacton train, and there was nothing for it but to wait along with the rest and hope it didn't take too long to get a train. We always stayed at the same place in a B&B, and the lady there had a black spaniel called Bess. I loved to walk Bess as I had never had a pet so volunteered whenever there was an opportunity.

Mum and Dad would not come on the beach. As they were so much older than the average parents, they were concerned not to get any sand in their socks/stockings and so sat on the promenade whilst I went and played on my own on the beach. The salt water was supposed to be good for my skin, as were the UV rays on that coast, and I think that was why we always went there every year. It was certainly true that my skin did improve greatly and was generally much better by the time we went home. It was also one of the nearest seaside places to Chelmsford in Essex, and we sometimes met up with Mum's relatives who lived there. Sometimes they came to Clacton for the day, and on those occasions we did sit on the sand all together. I have an old photo of my aunt and uncle and their three girls together with us on the beach. The photo also includes my sister Beryl, and Nan, my mum's mother.

Nan and Grandad lived in Writtle, Essex, where he was a pastor at a small congregational chapel. We visited on a couple of rare occasions, and I was intrigued at their home. They had a kitchen with flagged stone floor and an old kitchen range that had to be black-leaded and stoked with fuel winter and summer. On the floor were rugs made of old rags, and I learned how to make such a rug from a piece of sackcloth and old cut-up strips of material. There was no electricity at all; they used oil lamps downstairs, and upstairs we had a candle. It was fun trying to get a noise out of the old church organ, and you had to push the pedals like mad to get enough wind for it to make a sound. In later years, after Grandad had died, Nan came to live with the family, spending a few months at each of the family in turn. Nan lived until she was ninety-one.

CHAPTER TWO

Teens

BEFORE LEAVING JUNIOR SCHOOL, EVERY CHILD HAD TO learn their twelve times tables by rote and we were tested on these and also spellings every week. Mental arithmetic was considered a good skill to have, remembering that before decimalisation there were twelve pence in every shilling and twenty shillings in a pound. In those days everyone took the exam called the 11+, and this enabled entry to a grammar school. On passing my exam, I had a choice of schools and chose Cheney Secondary Technical School which was a co-educational school. This school was quite a few miles away, and I either took the bus or in good weather rode my bicycle. The cycle ride was quite long and through what I thought was busy traffic, although probably nowhere near as hazardous as it would be today. There was the choice of riding up Headington Hill or Southfields, a similar hill but more of a long drag and not quite so steep. Riding to school was fine, but I did develop some good leg muscles that, when I stopped riding, turned to fat. How I envied girls with slim legs, and I remember a most embarrassing moment in a dress shop when trying on a dress and hearing a derogatory comment from someone in the next cubicle. Mum and Dad did not believe in diets, and I was quite chubby as a youngster – not surprising on a diet of rice pudding, mashed potato and lots of pastry.

My mum was a good pastry cook and there was never a shortage of jam tarts and mince pies. Dad liked old-fashioned food so we never had anything different. Meat and veg and fish and mash – potatoes with everything. No wonder I'm not a fan of potatoes very much. Chips were unheard of at home, and I never knew there was such a thing as a fish and chips shop until we went on holiday at Clacton.

Because water and handling flour were not good for my skin, I was not allowed to help with the cooking so sadly grew up without a most basic skill of being able to cook. We did learn cooking (domestic science) at senior school however, albeit very simple things. An embarrassing accident occurred one day following our cookery lesson... I had made 'bananas and custard', of all things, and had to take this culinary effort home in a jar. At the end of the school day, the bell rang and we all piled into the corridor. In the jostling, I completely lost hold of the jar and dropped it. The contents spilled out all over the corridor floor right at the feet of a senior teacher! Not my best moment.

About the time I was thirteen we moved house to Marston. The bakery had been taken over by another company but they allowed us to remain in the house provided we paid rent. Dad got another job as a night watchman at Cowley car plant and we continued to live there. However, eventually the new owners wanted the property for their workers and so they offered us another rental house in Marston. For the first time, we actually had a proper bathroom and we were really pleased. It was also around that time that my sister Beryl got married, and I was again a bridesmaid, this time a little better behaved.

I enjoyed senior school more than juniors as I made some nice friends. We used to spend a lot of breaks playing five-stones and jacks, and I was able to visit my friend's house. I found to my surprise that I could sing and joined the choir. I really enjoyed singing practice and was really happy to be involved in some school concerts and productions. One highlight was a production of *Ruddigore,* and I played Dame Hannah which was an alto part. The choir concerts were excellent and we entered a choir competition. One memorable concert was when I and others sang an old English madrigal acapella. I loved it.

P.E. was still a pain as I have never been athletic and especially hated cross-country running. My friend and I made a sorry duo coming last because we walked most of the way. I did enjoy tennis though, and the school had two teams that played in inter-school tournaments. I was in the second 'six' team for tennis. Amazingly, I also made the school hockey team as well, but as goalie! Yes, we had padded gloves and leg pads but no helmet or head protection, and I wore glasses. Thankfully, I never received any injuries from my goalie days.

Being a secondary technical school meant that the school was set up rather differently, and once completing the second year, each pupil had to choose a route through the remainder of the school. These were art subjects, technical subjects and commercial subjects. I chose commercial subjects and therefore, in addition to basic curriculum, also studied shorthand, typing, commerce and accounts. These were skills that enabled me to find work on leaving school as it meant I already had a qualification for RSA and Pitman's shorthand and typing. It was as a consequence of this choice that from then on I missed out on sciences and art subjects. Looking back, it was obviously geared to equip me for work, but there have been great areas missing from my education.

The school entered us for GCE 'O' levels and I took eight subjects. The time leading up to these exams was stressful and this showed itself in my eczema flaring up again. How I hated going to school in bandages! Because I did well at my subjects, one teacher suggested I might stay on at school to do 'A' levels, but I was so embarrassed and unhappy that all I could think about was leaving. So I left school at sixteen and got a job in a bank in the city centre.

So where was God and how did I relate to him in my early years? Mum joined the Baptist Church and I went to Sunday school there. A sweet elderly lady used to encourage me to believe in Jesus, but I resisted and only went along because Mum wanted me to and it never occurred to me to disobey her. I still have the book *Kenilworth* which was given to me as a prize for attendance when I was thirteen. However, I was quite resentful and used 'Xmas' on my Christmas Cards as a small protest. Walking to Sunday school on a Sunday afternoon was not without its hassle, as a group of local boys used to wait for me and verbally abuse me *en route*. I think the area where I lived was a downtrodden area, and the fact I had Sunday best clothes to wear to church made me a target for the bullies. Despite my parents never having a lot to spare, I was always bought a gabardine mackintosh for weekdays and a Sunday best coat. Admittedly, when new, they were always a size too big so that I could grow into them and then eventually replaced when I grew out of them. Coats were expensive and made to last as long as possible.

It was only slowly in my teens I began to be more receptive to the message of the gospel, and when a new minister came to the church, I found myself more drawn into activities. I especially liked the minister's wife and found I could talk to her. Several of my peers at the church were getting baptised, but I still resisted, saying it was not for me.

Then one night something peculiar happened. I was drifting off to sleep, and it was like I could see a figure standing at the foot of my bed. "I want you to be baptised," he said. "No," I said in my dream and went to sleep. This sequence repeated the next evening and again I said no. Then on the third night I said, "OK, I will."

I did not tell anyone of my odd experience but went to the minister's wife and told her I wished to be baptised. I cannot pinpoint a date for this but know that it was around the time I left school at the age of sixteen.

I attended a series of classes before my baptism so knew the basics of faith, but it was a mistake on the part of others in the church who immediately put me to work teaching the little children in the Sunday school. This meant I was taken out of Sunday morning worship and receiving teaching myself, and I did not have the self-discipline to read the Bible for myself and so did not grow.

I did, however, enjoy singing in the choir, and that was a very positive part of church. Every year the young people were involved in singing for the church anniversary and also every summer there would be a garden party in the grounds of a farm off the Abingdon Road. Pity the garden party was always at the height of the hay fever season, so the three-legged race and other games in the newly mown fields were not an option for me. The young people's group at that time also put on a couple of dramas/musicals. Close friendships never really happened for me at church, although my mum did have some nice friends through her involvement with the Ladies' Fellowship group of which she was the secretary.

On reflection now, I know God is outside of our time as we know it and sees the end from the beginning. What exactly transpired when I was baptised and professed faith in Christ, I am not theologically qualified to say, but I think He set His seal upon my life knowing what was going to happen in the ensuing years when I fell away. I don't know how things would have turned out if I had not said yes when I did.

Chapter Three

World of Work

AT SIXTEEN I COULDN'T WAIT TO LEAVE SCHOOL. AFTER all the swotting and anxiety, plus the bad eczema accompanying that, I was so glad to leave. With hindsight, I wish now that I had stayed to do 'A' levels; although initially it was good to be able to leave and get a job, later on in life when I tried to change to another career, I found out that it was a big obstacle.

My shorthand and typing skills gave me an entry into office work and, as I mentioned earlier, my first job was at the city bank. In those days the bank opened on Saturday mornings; you had to arrive promptly in the morning and weren't allowed to go home at the end of the day until the tills balanced! I wanted to learn to be a cashier. My very first days of working at the bank were an education. Obviously, wanting to make a good impression, I turned up dressed in my smart 'working in the office' clothes, only to be sent upstairs to the filthy dirty attic for three days searching for old cheques among the hundreds of bundles up there. Old cheques were kept for years in case of a subsequent query, and as the new girl, I was given the job no-one else wanted to do.

After that I went on a course to learn basic banking skills which involved lots of practice at adding up long columns of figures at speed. I never did get to work on the counters at the bank, however. I did spend some time on entering clients' transactions on statements, all of which were done manually, but once they realised I had shorthand and typing skills, I was put in the secretary's office. I soon realised that other banking jobs were now passing me by and, because of the poor pay, I began looking for a secretarial job elsewhere that paid properly for the skills and qualification I had. I did make a few friends among the younger staff there, one of whom turned out to be my future husband, Keiran.

I had a job interview lined up at the local government offices. The Saturday evening before, Keiran and I and our small group of friends went out into the countryside and enjoyed a BBQ and sat around the fire talking for quite a while. When we got up to make our way home, we suddenly realised that a fog had come up without us realising and we were in the middle of a pea souper. I was riding pillion on Keiran's lambretta scooter, and the journey home proved quite tricky trying to follow the edge of the grassy bank on the side of the road. Suddenly, the grass verge disappeared, the scooter slid and we fell off. We were not seriously hurt, but I injured my ankle and had a sizeable hole where I had obviously landed on a stone or something sharp. Early the next morning was a trip to A&E at the infirmary, and they bound it up for me, gave me a crutch and said not to walk on it too much to give it time to heal. That was all very well, but I had a job interview on Monday morning and did not intend to miss it. So I did attend the interview, bandaged foot and all, and got the job.

I worked for one of the departmental heads, and the offices were on the third floor. The offices were newly built, and it was a few weeks before we had any proper heating. I shared an office with three other typists, and it was quite funny that you were allotted some carpet with the size according to your rank. Each typist had a very small square of carpet under the desk, just enough to put your feet on; the deputy head had a small office with a bit bigger bit of carpet; and the boss had a much bigger office and a much bigger bit of carpet. Oh the hierarchy – with standard desks and chairs, how else could we tell to whom we should bow?! These were the days of back-combing and bouffant hair styles, and I remember a girl called Donna whose black hair stood a good six or eight inches off the top of her head. It was lacquered so stiff that she only washed it and re-lacquered it once a week. In between it never moved an inch. She was a great laugh, and I wonder whatever happened to her in later life.

Although I didn't work in the bank any more, I still went out with Keiran and the same group of friends. By this time we were living in Marston and I went to work each day on the bus. The buses were very frequent, and after work I would stand in a long queue to wait for a bus home. They were supposed to be every ten minutes, but sometimes we waited fifteen or twenty minutes, then two would come along together. That became such a common occurrence, it became a joke. Most people used the bus in those days, as running a car was a luxury most people could not afford.

One of the things Keiran and I often did was to walk from Marston through the University Parks to St Giles, have a burger at Wimpy and then get the bus back to Marston. Then he would catch the bus back again and catch the last bus to his home. In these days of jumping into a car it seems strange, but we thought nothing of it as that was our way of life then. The group of friends we went around with were Jean, who worked in the bank; John, who was a salesman but later joined the Metropolitan Police; Annie and Mick, both of whom were into ballroom dancing; Phil, and Maggie, who was a typist at the police station; and another friend studying to be a doctor. We were a motley lot and used to meet up and go to the pub for a drink. The lads would take it in turns to buy rounds of drinks, and I used to think nothing of downing four 'gin and it' (Gin and Vermouth) during the course of an evening.

Keiran and I got engaged when I was nineteen years old; he too had left the bank and signed up for the local police force. My parents were not happy and insisted that I waited to get married until I was twenty-one. Twenty-one was the age of becoming an adult then, and before that I needed my parents' permission, which they would not give. At the time I found it hard to appreciate their stand, but I think now that probably my mum was not happy that Keiran was not a Christian and the Bible tells us very clearly, "Do not be yoked together with an unbeliever." Sadly, because I was not reading the Bible for myself, I did not know that and she never actually told me the real reason for their objection. However, being young and headstrong, I doubt whether I would have listened anyway. So we were engaged for two years and during that time I saved as much money as I could so that we would be able to buy some furniture for our prospective home. All of Keiran's spare money went to paying the HP on his scooter.

It never ceases to amaze me that today couples seem to have everything when they start off making a home together, and what is more, that is their expectation. In the sixties we had to save for every stick of furniture, and I was always mindful of one of my dad's favourite 'Norfolk' sayings – "neither a lender nor a borrower be". HP (short for hire purchase) was easy enough to get, just as a credit card and other loans are today, but with a very limited income, they posed a great danger to be avoided if at all possible.

The indoctrination of my father's principles have remained with me throughout life. I am mindful that years before, when his bakery business went bust, he insisted on paying back every creditor, unlike businesses today where debts are written off and liquidation is sometimes used as a means of avoiding liabilities. It is very true that the things we learn in our youth stay with us throughout future years.

CHAPTER FOUR

Marriage and Babies

WHEN I FIRST GOT TO KNOW KEIRAN, HE DID LEAD ME TO think he was used to going to church and told me he had been christened and confirmed. He did come with me to church on a very few occasions, but of course that ceased once we were married. My faith had seriously backslidden by this time, but I was still conscious enough of God to want to have my wedding in the Baptist Church where I had grown up and where my mum still belonged. Because I worked for the local council, I managed to book the reception in at the Oxford town hall. The town hall had a significant entrance with quite a large number of stairs leading up to the reception rooms, and that day I did feel like royalty standing at the top of the stairs receiving my guests. We honeymooned on the Isle of Wight at Shanklin and travelled there on the train and ferry. Our friends made quite a mess of the train carriage with confetti etc., but we changed trains and left the other occupants of the train to take the brunt of the complaints on arrival at Paddington.

Our first home was a police house. Our next door neighbour was also a policeman in the city force and a dog handler. His Alsatian police dog lived in a kennel in the back garden, and when he went on holiday, another dog handler used to come to feed him. The local tradespeople were very wary about visiting the house, as it had been known for one of them to be pinned up against the wall. One summer day, while the officer was away on holiday, the dog got out and was sunning himself on the front lawn. We were obviously worried, but Keiran quickly got in touch with another dog handler, who came to get him back into his pen. The handlers were supplied with the best steak for the dogs, and sometimes we used to think the dog ate better than we did. We enjoyed ourselves, and thoughts of God and my walk with Him slipped away little by little.

I moved jobs again and went to work at the polytechnic. This was a college of further education situated virtually next door geographically to my old secondary school. I worked as a secretary to the registrar i.e. chief administrator. He was an older and rather rotund man with a permanent sun tan. I later learned he had been a policeman in India when he lived there during the old 'British' rule and still had that air about him of colonialism. He was a very pleasant person, and I liked him and his wife. They had a wonderful house overlooking open fields on the outskirts of the city, and even after I had left and he had retired, I occasionally visited them there. The polytechnic was a good place to work, and I gained some knowledge about several departments. On the whole the engineers were the most 'down to earth' and the Architecture Department the most academic, far too elevated to speak to the likes of me. Edward Bailey worked in the Engineering Department and it was many years later on that I became friends with him and his wife Ruby, whom I worked with at social services. Whilst working at the polytechnic I gained further qualifications in typing and word processing, as this was around the time the first computers and word processors were invented.

I stayed at the college until I was pregnant with my first baby, and Lizzie was born in March 1967. Keiran was doing a stint working on the police traffic department and regularly rode a police motorcycle. As the time for the birth approached, we had no phone and he was working nights. Our arrangement was that he would ride past the house approximately once an hour if possible, and if the bedroom light was on, he would call in. My labour was a hasty affair, and once things really got going, I needed to be at the GP Unit attached to the hospital pretty quickly. That is the one time Keiran drove over the Headington traffic lights with his foot down. The gift of a child is so amazing and so special, and arriving home from the hospital is a pretty special moment. I believed in being at home for my babies and so I did not attempt to return to working full-time at the college. Nowadays people's mortgage and rent commitments are so high that, sadly, they cannot have that luxury of choice. I realise now that spending those pre-school years with the children was an amazing gift. In those days the mortgage company would only loan three times the husband's salary as a maximum on the assumption that the wife would not be working. So until my girls started school, I was a stay-at-home mum. Some typing work at home brought in a little extra money, and I was happy to help the organiser at the polytechnic who managed their entry for the BBC programme *Young Scientist of the Year.*

Once the mortgage was paid each month, we had very little money but were very happy. I used to have a tin box where I apportioned set amounts of money each month in order to pay the bills. Direct debits that we have today did not exist, and I had to be responsible in paying bills on time. At the end of the month the cash in hand would run out, and so I would take some money from the tin box and put an IOU in its place. On payday it would be replaced, and we would hope that next month would be better. There was no spare cash for extras, it was hard enough paying for essentials, but we didn't get into debt. Laughingly, I tell those who will listen how I bought 1 lb (400g) beef mince, mixed it with potato, swede and carrots, and made twenty-four Cornish pasties, enough to last us several meals. And this was the young lady who had never learned to cook!

Jane was born in 1970, another beautiful girl. Again I had an easy pregnancy and birth; I did not have any stitches with either birth and was told "it was like shelling peas". (Well, I suppose that's one compensation for having wide hips.) I was so proud of my "little girls" and I have remained proud of them all through their lives. They have been the best thing that ever happened to me, and I thank God for them all the time; they are so precious.

As I said, the gift of a new life is amazing. When I looked at my babies and saw their perfectly formed limbs, even to the tiny fingernails, I had to acknowledge God's creation is amazing. Sadly, I was so caught up in nappies and daily life that God was again squeezed out of my daily experience.

In the Bible it says, "Can a mother forget the baby at her breast and have no compassion on the child she has borne? Though she may forget, I will not forget you."[2]

---

[2] Isaiah 49:15

How precious that thought is now, that although I forgot God and let everything else take precedence over Him, He did not forget me.

While the children were young, our social life was very limited. Some dear friends, Mary and Dave, who also had two girls of similar age, used to get a babysitter and come for the evening. The 'fellas' had a firkin of beer, and we used to play Canasta (a card game, for those uninitiated). It could be quite a lengthy game and used to take up most of the evening. We had met Mary and Dave on a week's holiday at a facility chosen due to the fact it had a baby monitoring system. Keiran recognised Mary as they had attended the same senior school and it turned out they still lived locally. Mary and Dave had a two-year-old daughter and we really hit it off and became firm friends.

I was able to continue my love of singing with the Operatic Society and was always pleased to be involved in their yearly productions at the Playhouse Theatre. I have great memories of being part of their productions – *Iolanthe, Yeoman of the Guard* and others, which were great fun. Today you would find it hard to believe that as part of the chorus in *Die Fledermaus* I danced the can-can. We met all through the year to learn the music and rehearse, and then the exciting day would come when we took over the Oxford Playhouse Theatre for the week's production. Those with leading roles would have the 'star' dressing rooms on the ground floor, the ladies' chorus used dressing rooms on the first floor, and the men's chorus had one large communal dressing room on the top floor. Singing was thirsty work and it was the norm for everyone to pile into the men's dressing room for the interval, where we would share their crate of beer. Until singing with the operatic, I never liked beer and thought it tasted awful, but after a week of joining in with their jollities, I found I did have a taste for beer after all.

A memorable holiday was one year when we were able to use a caravan belonging to an aunt of mine and go to the seaside. It's funny how music and tunes stick in your mind; just then the favourite song for the girls was 'Itzy bitzy teeny weeny yellow polka dot bikini'. I would not like to say I'm completely sure, but I think that holiday was a revisit to Clacton on Sea, a reminder of my holidays as a child.

It is said that the only thing that's certain is change. It was in 1974 that things changed dramatically when Keiran was offered a job as a police sergeant in the new Thames Valley Force. He had studied for his sergeant's exams, and I had helped as much as I could by giving him time and space for study and keeping him going with endless cups of coffee. We both felt a sense of achievement when he passed, and whether he admitted it or not, I knew I had contributed by looking after the house and children so that he could study in peace.

We looked at the towns where he might be posted and thought that Bracknell would be OK. We were right in our assumption and it proved a good place to live. We moved just as Jane started school as a rising five in the October of that year, and both girls went to the local infants and junior schools. We moved into a four-bedroom semi-detached house just under a mile away from the schools.

Because I was not concerned about God or His plan for my life, I happily embarked on this new adventure. Yes, it was sad leaving my parents behind, and I knew that they would miss the girls dreadfully, but it was also exciting to move to a new place. All the while I had ignored God, my mum had faithfully taken the girls with her to church and to the Sunday school, and it was her commitment that finally made a significant change once we moved away.

CHAPTER FIVE

Meeting God After Fifteen Years

DURING THE YEARS WHEN I HAD LAPSED IN MY ATTEND-
ance at church, my mother had continued her faithful love of Christ
and was involved in her church. As I said before, she was a secretary
for the Women's Fellowship and for several years was at the centre of
that group, serving God there. She was also a very generous person,
and I remember her always bringing treats for the children when they
were little and enjoying our little trips to the swings and to feed the
ducks. I never ceased to be amazed that such a lovely and generous
person could be married for so long to such a mean and
uncommunicative man. It is sad for me to realise now that I knew very
little of their feelings and how they had obviously had to work at their
marriage throughout the years.

And so, as I said, back in Oxford when I no longer went to church,
my mum used to take the children with her to Sunday school. In any
case, I was always of the opinion that every adult should be able to
make informed choices and that without some religious input, my girls
would not be able to make their own choice later in life for themselves.
So it was that when we moved to Bracknell, my girls were in the habit
of going to church each Sunday. It was quite scary moving to a new
location where I knew no-one, and I decided that taking the girls to
Sunday school might be a way of getting to meet people. Of course,
we no longer had a ready-made babysitter, and I felt this acutely as it
seriously curtailed our lifestyle. That is how I started to attend Christ
Church.

Rex met me at the door with a cheerful welcome – it was nice to
see a friendly face. He later told me that the minister had been primed
from Oxford to look out for me, a young mum with two little girls

and a non-Christian husband. Thank you, Mum, for sending word ahead.

And so, as I sat week after week listening to the minister spell out the gospel, I began to feel uncomfortable. For one thing, I had always thought erroneously that everyone went to heaven, and for another, I began to realise the seriousness of my sins and old way of life. In my younger days at Oxford, I had listened to intellectual sermons mostly aimed at the undergraduates in the university, and I must confess to not understanding a lot of the content. Now I began to understand in plain English that I was a sinner and I needed Christ.

All this took place during the period of October 1974 to March 1975, and one week I took courage and asked to see the minister to talk about my situation. I told him that God was convicting me of my sins, however I had already been baptised at Oxford when I was sixteen. Now at the age of thirty-one, I wanted a fresh start. Following that conversation, I prayed and asked Jesus to forgive me of all my sins and make me clean again. I asked him to be my personal saviour and committed my life to him afresh.

Now I knew what people meant when they said they were 'born again Christians'! I had never before felt such joy and acceptance and a sense of being clean. I cried tears of happiness, and that day Jesus changed my life.

All of a sudden, I was hungry to read the Bible, and started going to a study group for new Christians. As I learned more about God's plan of salvation, my sense of wonder grew, and my love and commitment for Jesus grew also. Church became a joy, and I looked forward each week to Sunday mornings. I still couldn't go on a Sunday evening because Keiran looked upon that as "over the top" – he was not very pleased about my newfound faith, and although he didn't spell it out at the time, I felt his antagonism. Later on, I discovered that he thought I was a "religious nutcase".

I became friends with Jacky, another lady in the church who had a non-believing husband. She and I engaged in door-to-door evangelism in the north of the town. Keiran knew about this and OK'd it, provided I didn't do it anywhere near where any of his friends or colleagues lived; in other words, he was ashamed of me and didn't want his police colleagues knowing anything about it. The church scheme was to first of all put through the door letters of introduction and then to follow this up with a personal visit a couple of weeks later. We mostly met refusals, but there were two or three people who met with us, one of whom was Isabella who was Spanish. Another Christian lady whom we met offered us her apartment so that we could meet together, and I was given the task of preparing a topic for us to discuss. This was very new to me and I felt totally inadequate where to begin, so I prayed. God answers prayer and he led me to look at 1 Corinthians 15:35-56 where the passage tells us about what happens after death. When I arrived at the get-together with Isabella, it turned out that was just the very topic she wanted to ask about. I was so encouraged – God had heard my prayer and answered in a very real way.

Isabella became a friend, and Amelia her daughter became friends with Lizzie and Jane and started to attend church. Amelia later made a commitment to Christ and is still in touch with Lizzie, who has remained her friend over the years. However, Isabella was Roman Catholic by her upbringing and lacking in knowledge of what the Bible says. She was very superstitious and it was hard for her to understand what knowing Jesus was all about. She was a lovely and generous person, and I hope and pray one day she will come to know Jesus for herself.

And so began twenty years at Christ Church and, more importantly, years of following Jesus and discovering his will for my life. My love of singing now had a new outlet; now I wanted to sing God's praises. I remembered a song learned as a small child in the Sunday school at Oxford and have used that little song as the theme for this book:

> *Jesus bids us shine,*
> *With a pure, clear light,*
> *Like a little candle,*
> *Burning in the night.*
> *In this world is darkness,*
> *We must shine –*
> *You in your small corner,*
> *And I in mine.*

CHAPTER SIX

Family Life

NOW THAT WE LIVED IN BRACKNELL, AS I ALREADY SAID, we were lacking babysitters. Keiran's dad had died of lung cancer just before Jane was born, and Keiran's mum lived north of Oxford in a little village called Fringford. She was in her seventies and did not drive, so Keiran would go and fetch her to stay with us every couple of months or so. She used to come for the weekend, and that enabled her to have a break with us and also for us to have an evening out on our own.

Granny was a lively, cheerful and kindly person. She was a quiet believer and I knew she prayed for us and attended her local C of E church. The children loved her to come and stay as that meant that they could get into her bed first thing in the morning at about 6 am and have stories read to them. Although she had a male friend in the village, Granny had decided not to marry again. She told me that she had buried two husbands and that she didn't want to have to look after any more sick people. She herself had good health, although she did take pills for her blood pressure.

It was during this time we inherited 'King', a rough collie. Keiran brought him home as his colleague had decided to have the dog put down due to his habit of wandering off. I had been afraid of large dogs as a child and thought it might be a good idea, as I wanted the girls to be able to be around dogs. When King arrived, he was much larger than I had imagined and my thought was that he looked like a lion getting out of the car. He pined for his original owner for three weeks and wouldn't eat anything. In the end we tempted him with chocolate – Mars bars, marshmallows, Wagon Wheels etc. King finally accepted us, having been softened up by his sweet tooth, and became part of the family.

Jane was very nervous of him at first but got used to him, and the girls were easy with him. I remember their first attempts at taking him for a walk; Lizzie and Jane took King for a little excursion up the road and came back reporting that he had done dozens of 'wees'. I never totally trusted King, as he could unexpectedly snap and he could be very stubborn, but he was a good family pet and came with us on some holidays. One caravan holiday when we took King with us, he was very friendly with some of the other campers. We found out at the end of the week that he had been eating his dinner with us, then going along to another family to get fed all over again by them! "He had such a sad face," they told us – just goes to show appearances can be deceptive.

The girls settled well into school, which was only a fifteen-minute walk away but involved crossing a main road with fast-moving traffic. I used to walk them to school each day, including walking up to meet them at lunchtime so that they could come home for dinner, then walking them back again, and lastly collecting them at the end of the school day. Every journey King accompanied us and thus, with eight fifteen-minute walks each day, got his exercise, although I also used to take him to a farmer's field near to our home. It's surprising what sticks in your memory, and two more culinary disasters come to mind. Jane wrote about my rock cakes in her school book and said, "Mummy made some cakes and they were *rook* hard." About that time we also purchased one of the newly invented microwaves and my first attempt at a cake resulted in a discus-like object which we used as a frisbee to play in the garden!

I was becoming more involved in Christ Church and attended a small ladies' group one morning a week. I felt full of joy and excitement at knowing Jesus at last and wanted to join in as much as I could. Of course, I had to limit the times I was away from Keiran in case he should feel neglected. My friend Jacky also had a non-Christian husband and her situation was fairly similar, so we had a lot in common. It was a great shame that Keiran thought he was a Christian already just because he had sung in the choir when he was a small boy and been confirmed in the Church of England. He didn't see any need to have God in his day-to-day life.

Although I was keen and exploring my newfound faith, I still had an occasion of unbelief... I had visitors for tea one day and tried to open a bottle of something; just what was the contents were escapes my memory, but what I do remember is trying my hardest to open it without success. It was firmly stuck and no-way could I open it. In my frustration I spoke a prayer: "God, if you are really there, please open this bottle for me." At once the top became loose in my hands, and a voice whispered in my ear: "Do not tempt the Lord your God." I was amazed at the stupidity of what I had just done and then doubly amazed that God had so graciously answered.

Lizzie and Jane were involved in the Brownie Pack, and I became a helper. Janice was Brown Owl and Sue was Tawny Owl. I became Wise Owl – because I wore glasses! Brownies was great fun; it was an openly Christian pack and we always had a waiting list of girls to join.

Jumping forward, after some years we embarked on 'Pack Holidays'. This meant taking a group of twenty-four girls away to a fairly local venue – usually in a wooden hut or small hall, not under canvas. The week was carefully planned to include a variety of activities every day and encouraged the girls in social skills, team building and basic home skills. Even in those days we had to plan meticulously with a leader, first aider, a cook and helpers. The week was themed and each of the helpers became a character from the stories. One year in particular was themed 'Winnie the Pooh' and by this time I had taken over the job of Brown Owl. Of course, we had to be in costume as much as possible, and my garb was a red T-shirt with the name 'Pooh' written in large yellow letters. This was fine until we took the pack for an outing and were walking around the local shopping centre, the girls calling loudly to me, "Poooooh! Pooooh!" The Brownies were divided into teams (Sixes) for competitive purposes to encourage participation, effort and team loyalty and they were awarded stars and points for good behaviour and results. I was amazed at the number of girls who had never peeled a potato or done any washing-up. Well, they soon learned! Later on Lizzie became a dedicated Guider and completed almost all her badges required to become a Queen's Guide. It was quite an achievement.

Now that both girls were older and happily settled in school, they were able to take a packed lunch and I began to look for work. My journey back to work began with a part-time office job at the Electricity Board offices. I used to walk there through a small woodland as it was a shortcut provided you were on foot. Today the woodland is not entirely safe to walk in on your own, but in those days there was little to be afraid of and I was quite at ease walking through the woods to work.

One day I had an extraordinary experience on the way to work. I was walking quite briskly through the wood and singing, just praising God for the beauty of His creation. I found that once I became a Christian, all of nature seemed to have brighter colours than before and the beauty of the morning and the woodland was just amazing. As I just lifted up my praise to God, all of a sudden I heard him speak to me. He said, "Be still and know that I am God." I was so surprised, I stood stock still in my tracks and heard nothing else, but, as I stood there, I had a sensation of being hugged and completely covered as if wrapped in a warm blanket. It was a very special moment and one I will always treasure.

Subsequently, I worked as a secretary in the School of Art. This was in an old school building on the road almost opposite the church. My main concern was that my working hours would fit in with the school day, and I always wanted to make sure that I would be able to collect the girls at home time. My position was as secretary to the head, and it surprised me that he agreed to my leaving the office at 3 pm each day (must have been a God fix). Anyway, I was pleased to get the job and enjoyed it. One thing I was particularly pleased about was that I found a piano teacher who lived just a couple of minutes' walk away, and I was able to see her in my lunch break one day a week to try to resume my interest in piano skills.

Now, after many years, I had finally come to appreciate the opportunity I had missed in learning piano, and when we moved to Bracknell, I took with me Mum's old piano which she graciously let me have. It was an upright piano with a case made of rosewood, and we put it in our large sitting room. Having wood block floors made it easy to move; the only thing was, I had to put little cups of water inside it to combat the effects of the central heating, which it was not used to. A couple of the notes didn't play which was very frustrating, and also I had it tuned but it was so old that it didn't stay in tune. I was happy to have a second try at learning and took exams up to grade five. It was disappointing; my teacher retired at this point and moved away to Worthing on the south coast. I tried to keep going on my own, but again my self-discipline was lacking and I let it slide. The fact that I was now working and keeping house for the four of us contributed to the lack of time, but I am sad that I let this slide for want of effort and dedication.

Things seemed to be fine for a while. I was enjoying my work, my family and my newfound faith. Keiran's niece got married in July 1976, and Lizzie and Jane were bridesmaids. They were very excited about the dressing up in posh frocks and they had their hair curled for the occasion. Jane's hair, of course, was naturally wavy and so held her curls for the duration, but Lizzie's hair was naturally straight and so during the day her curls tended to fall out. But they both looked very pretty and did their duties as bridesmaids admirably. Towards the end of the reception, Jane was getting quite tired and so I fed her sugar lumps to give her some energy to keep going.

One weekend the art school had a fire. I received a phone call to wear old clothes to work on Monday and arrived to find everything blackened and soot-covered. We relocated to an old unused school building west of Bracknell and continued there for some time. I learned to ride a moped and used it to go to work, until one icy day I travelled across the school playground to park the bike and got off, only to slip over because the whole playground was like a sheet of glass with solid ice. Things were not the same, and we never did return to the original building, which later became a home for another local government department.

Now I was earning, we had some proper holidays and went to Guernsey a couple of times, staying at Cobo Bay. We enjoyed that, and I especially liked the time we saw the flower festival in St Peter Port and Saumarez Park. That was really spectacular. Granny also came on holiday with us one year along with King.

Family times together were special, my girls were so precious and everything seemed good, perhaps too good to last...

CHAPTER SEVEN

Family Grief

PHYLLIS DIED OF A BRAIN TUMOUR IN THE AUTUMN OF 1978. She was fifty-three years old. She had been having bad headaches for a few years and they were increasing. As time went on, these headaches would put her to bed for a couple of days. Then her eyesight began to deteriorate and she had tunnel vision. All the while, the doctors said she was suffering from migraines. Eventually, the doctors finally did some tests and discovered the brain tumour in September that year. Ken had to make a decision for her about surgery and he gave permission for them to operate. It was a delicate operation and the tumour was removed, but it grew again within ten days with a new ferocity and very quickly she was back where she started, only worse. She was moved to the hospice and she lived for another week or so. Eventually, she was unconscious, although the staff said that as hearing is the last thing to go, she possibly could have heard us as we visited her.

I was so upset. I knew Phyllis had made a commitment to Christ in her younger years, but since marrying Ken who was an atheist, she had not been to church and not expressed anything at all concerning her faith or lack of faith. I wanted to speak to her so badly, but every time I visited, Ken was there, and his demeanour was so threatening that I didn't dare speak to her about Jesus. He even denied her a visit from the hospital chaplain. All I could do was pray. When Phyllis finally died, I asked to be able to see her body. I'm glad I did, because as I looked at her, it was just like looking at an empty shell; the person inside had gone. I missed her and grieved for her; sometimes I would walk King and just cry. Ken too was devastated – he and Phyllis had not had any children and they were a very close couple. I used to phone him every evening, and he told me afterwards that this was his lifeline as he was so sad, he really wanted just to kill himself. It was so sad they had not had any children, as I know Phyllis would have made such a good mother. Apparently, she had had some miscarriages and even got to the point of adopting but then backed out at the last minute because she didn't have the confidence in herself. Phyllis and Ken had always been so good to me; I loved her very much.

However, something happened to make things very different. As I said, I used to often cry when I was walking King and thinking about Phyllis. One day I was taking King across the farmer's field towards the tunnel of trees on the far side, when again I heard God speaking to me. He said, "Don't cry; she is with me. Tell Ken and he will know that I am God." How glad I was to hear those words; it was what I needed to know, the assurance that Phyllis was with God and not lost forever. I did tell Ken – repeating the words exactly. I don't know what impact the words had on him, but in later years he did express a faith in God to me, an amazing turnaround for an atheist!

My mum died of a stroke almost exactly a year later, in the autumn of 1979 – she was eighty-one years old. She was reasonably mobile, although she was slowing up, of course, and showing signs of age. She never really got over Phyllis's death. The first stroke she had was very slight and her recovery quick. The second one put her in hospital, and she lost the use of one side but could still talk OK. It was upsetting to see the nurses put her food in front of her and then leave her to get on with it, when she obviously had a problem feeding herself. She was worried about coming home as it was obvious that Dad wouldn't cope. She had looked after him for years, but I really couldn't see that he would be able to look after her.

In the event, any decision to be taken was not needed, as a third stroke about ten days later put her in a coma and she never regained consciousness. I think it was God's mercy to take her; she would have been very unhappy not being able to get about and having to rely on others all the time, and especially as Dad would have found it very difficult. Mum was a lovely Christian lady, generous and kind and always ready to help if she could. I was glad she was most certainly with God, and I chose the words for her tombstone 'Forever with the Lord'. One day when I die, I will meet Phyllis and Mum again, and I hope that I will also meet Ken too. How precious is our hope in the gospel: "For God so loved the world that he gave his one and only Son, that whoever believes in him shall not perish but have eternal life."[3]

---

[3] John 3:16

CHAPTER EIGHT

Divorce

I ALSO WORKED AT THE LOCAL COLLEGE OF FURTHER education as an administrator, but suffice it to say that by the spring of 1980, I had been at home for a year or so. I had had a problem with a tooth which had decayed, and the dentist recommended that I should have it crowned. Unfortunately, it was at the front and showed badly. Keiran got very uptight when the temporary crown I had fell off and I was 'gappy' for a few days until I got it fixed again. Once the real crown was fitted, it was fine and has lasted to this day. I should have taken more notice that Keiran seemed very preoccupied with looks. Because I was not going to work, I did not 'dress up' or 'make up', and although I was not slovenly, my ordinary everyday clothes were just that: ordinary. Of course, I paid attention to my looks on Sunday and when we went out or had visitors, but that was not every day.

Another clue I should have noticed was that when we went to a police 'do', he would laugh at the often rude and anti-God jokes and was very put out if I went to 'powder my nose'. He said I was being prudish because I didn't laugh at crudity. I suppose that taking our previous years in Oxford into account, he couldn't understand the change in me. Yes, I had changed – God was changing me – and I didn't fit into his idea of an ideal partner any more. Homemaking and caring for the children's needs were high on my priorities. I always worked hard and he worked hard too, and I was expected to 'play hard' as the saying goes.

Plain clothes policing meant that I didn't necessarily know when he was coming home. He sometimes worked late, and although I never realised at the time, it was a perfect cover for him to play away from home. I trusted him and didn't think he would use this to cheat on me – how wrong I was.

It was on a journey back home from his mother's that Keiran plucked up the courage to tell me he wanted a divorce. We were side by side in the front of the car; he couldn't even tell me to my face. It so happened I had an interview for a new job planned for the next day, and he said to me, "I should try and get that job if I were you." When I asked why he should say that, he said he was leaving me. I was in a state of shock and I just prayed, "Dear Lord, please help me." For the next week I functioned on autopilot and I lost half a stone in weight.

I don't know how I coped with the job interview. I went along and prayed that they wouldn't ask me any questions about my circumstances at home. I got the job and started work, again at the college of further education. It was only part-time hours and the money was not very much.

When I surfaced from this physical reaction, Keiran and I talked about things. He admitted he had had various liaisons and had now met someone whom he wanted to marry.

I wasn't going to give up that easily, and for several weeks I took every opportunity I could to talk to Keiran, to talk things through to make sure he knew what he was doing and what he really wanted. Our good friend Dave, bless him, also spent some time talking to Keiran and tried to persuade him otherwise. All this was to no avail, and it became a big strain talking and thinking and still trying to keep things 'normal' for the girls, who knew nothing of this. I didn't want them to know until it really happened, because I had a fantasy that if Keiran finally stayed, then they would never need to know.

About this time we both realised that we had booked a holiday for two weeks on the Gower Peninsula in a caravan. It was difficult. What should we do? Neither of us wanted to go, but the holiday had been booked for some time and the girls were looking forward to going to the seaside. In the end we agreed that we would go, and after one week Keiran could make the excuse that he was wanted for court and return home. Actually, what he did was to go to stay with his girlfriend for the week. I must have been a fool; I actually tried to give the girls as nice a holiday as I could without overspending on our budget, only to arrive home and find that Keiran had blown an exorbitant amount of money on living it up. I was cross, not only with him but with myself for being taken for a ride. All in all, that holiday was the worst time ever; I remember walking along the cliff with him and the girls and seriously contemplating stepping over the edge. It was only the thought "What would happen to my precious girls?" that stopped me.

Finally, I decided to talk to our church minister and pray together about what I should do. Keiran agreed to give me a few days to do this although he was itching to put the balls in motion. So I prayed and talked to Peter, who after some time pointed me to the verse in 1 Corinthians 7:13-15: "And if a woman has a husband who is not a believer and he is willing to live with her, she must not divorce him. For the unbelieving husband has been sanctified through his wife ... otherwise your children would be unclean, but as it is, they are holy. But if the unbeliever leaves, let it be so. The brother or sister is not bound in such circumstances; God has called us to live in peace."

This word seemed wise to me, so I told Keiran that while he remained living with me I would not divorce him. His response to this was to immediately pack his bags and leave. It was a great shock for the children, and thankfully, Granny was with us at the time. I agreed to be out of the house so that he could tell the girls; I went for a walk up the road, my mind in a turmoil, not knowing how things would work out, determined only to do the best I could for my darling girls, who didn't deserve any of this. When I returned, the girls and I hugged each other and we sat in a small circle and did some sewing. It seemed a strange thing to do but it seemed a way of coping to do *something*, anything.

Oh, I was so unhappy. "Dear Lord, why have You allowed this to happen?" The process of legal matters and solicitors was a blur. The house was in both our names, so I knew I was entitled to my half at least. My pride was hurt, and I decided I didn't want anything from Keiran that I wasn't entitled to. Other well-meaning people advised me that I could ask for more than my share, but I took just my half of the house, which was mine anyway, and an amount for maintenance until the girls left full-time education.

It felt like everything was totally overwhelming; I felt like I had never known Keiran, that the Keiran I had thought I knew had turned out to be someone else. I felt used and cast off like an old pair of shoes. I was angry that Keiran had only got his promotion because I had supported him and I had had all the lean years. My mind went back to the times when I would carefully budget our meagre monies to make them last the month; when I would go without things so that he and the girls could have clothes; when I would scrape a bit of money together to buy a few rolls of wallpaper! And yet we had been poor but happy; where had it all gone wrong? I blamed him; I blamed her; I blamed myself most of all. The lies and deceit hurt very much. What a fool I had been to trust him! And how I grieved for the children; Jane, especially, put her dad on a pedestal and became very withdrawn as a result of the split. Allowing the girls to spend time with their dad became a nightmare. I tried so hard not to say anything against him as I didn't want to poison their minds towards him. To let them go and see him was a wrench every time, and I likened it to a knife being thrust and turned in my stomach when I saw him face to face. I would walk down the street, screaming inside to people I saw passing by, "I'm getting divorced!" I felt shamed and unclean, unworthy and unlovable.

I was very touched by the people at church and their kindness, especially at Christmas when they sent me a gift of money from the church. Despite our poor finances, for the first time in my life I tithed my income and proved that God is no one's debtor. He provided for all our needs and we did not get into debt. The decree absolute came through in the spring of 1981, and Keiran married again that summer. I was thirty-eight.

It's inevitable when something like this happens that it splits not only the couple but families and friends. Keiran's cousin who lived in Cirencester all of a sudden wanted nothing to do with me and neither did the so called 'friends' in the police force. My only support was from Ken, Mary and Dave, and friends at church. To everyone else it was like I didn't exist any more. My sister Beryl saw me once for lunch, said I looked well and then didn't bother herself with me. When the chips are down, you find out who is really there for you.

God was there for me. Verses from Isaiah 43:1-5 became very precious: "But now this is what the LORD says, he who created you ... Fear not, for I have redeemed you; I have summoned you by name;

you are mine. When you pass through the waters I will be with you; and when you pass through the rivers, they will not sweep over you. When you walk through the fire you will not be burned; the flames will not set you ablaze. For I am the LORD, your God, the Holy One of Israel, your Saviour ... You are precious and honoured in my sight, and ... I love you. Do not be afraid, for I am with you." How I needed to hear those words "I love you", and what a comfort they were to me.

So life went on, and I worked as an administrator at the college. As Keiran had said, it was good that I had got myself some employment, otherwise we would have really struggled. The girls continued to do well at school, and I thanked God that their schoolwork had not suffered. They were both so good and such a help to me, I wanted to do all I could to make our daily lives as 'normal' as possible. They went to visit Keiran whenever he wanted them to, and this was very difficult. It was like reopening the wound which never seemed to heal. I know it was difficult for them too, especially Jane who used to get very nervous beforehand. I tried very hard not to run him down in any way as I knew it was important for them to still have respect for him as their father.

In those days the Child Support Agency did not exist and I was very dependent on Keiran to pay the maintenance we had agreed on. He was reliable and regular in his commitment to do this, for which I was grateful. Money was tight – but I had got years of experience of living on a tight budget and we managed. God is faithful and we always had enough.

Not only did I receive a gift of £50 from the church at Christmas, but also in the following year, when we went away on a church weekend at Northampton, the cost of that too was covered by someone else as a gift. God is true to his word. It was at this conference that I was baptised in the Holy Spirit and received a measure of healing. I cried on and off for three days after this event – some tears of healing, some tears of joy. The girls also received ministry for their hurt and received healing – it was a very special time. Of course, extending forgiveness featured large in this experience, and I have to admit it was an ongoing battle to be obedient to forgive and move on.

Another consequence was that I discovered that all of a sudden I was a threat to other couples because I was a divorcee, and also a target for men on the lookout. I prayed that I would find another man to love but that he would be a genuine Christian. My resolve was to never get involved with a non-Christian man again.

Sometimes strange supernatural things happen in your life that you think about afterwards and wonder about. Such an event was a small 'happening' when one day I was working in the front garden and a tall man in a long raincoat passed by. We lived in a cul-de-sac and I was familiar with the people who lived nearby or who walked their dogs to the farmer's field. I had never seen him before and yet he stopped and spoke to me and said I was to have hope because I would meet another man one day. He went off up the lane and I never saw him again. I thought and pondered this encounter; could he have been an angel sent to encourage me? Something about him made me think it a possibility.

Also, when years later I had met someone and shared with a friend who lived far away in Cornwall that I was about to be married again, she already knew that his name was George without my having told her. No-one else had told her either; there was no way she could have known this information beforehand. I felt God was confirming to me that the way forward was the right one.

There is a happy postscript to this story. Years later, in fact only in very recent years, Keiran has come to faith himself. One day I received a letter from him completely out of the blue, expressing his desire for forgiveness and telling me he was sorry for what happened. After so many years, this letter opened a can of worms for me that I had to work through, but I eventually came to the place I could freely and completely forgive and be glad for him that he had found the Lord Jesus for himself. Our God is truly amazing; I would have never believed that one day Keiran would become a Christian. Praise God!

CHAPTER NINE

Remarriage

ONE WINTER IN THE YEARS THAT FOLLOWED WAS exceptionally cold. My now elderly father who came initially to visit for Christmas ended up staying with me until March because his house was frozen up. He had been living alone since Mum died, and because the house in Marston had steep stairs and his mobility was not good, I offered him a home with me. And so it was that Dad came to live with me and the girls. My sister Beryl said I was a fool and that I could not rely on her for any help! Well, at least I knew where I stood.

After working at the college of further education for a while, I began to think about what I should be doing now that I was the main breadwinner. I thought of retraining and trying to get a proper career but I knew I also had to be earning money to maintain our home. The fact I did not have 'A' levels was in itself a hurdle, as I found I didn't meet the entry criteria. I pushed various doors and they did not open to me.

Eventually, I applied for a job at the Three Counties College in the office dealing with student registration and lodgings, and changed to full-time working. It was a different set-up at the college and it was not easy to get on with the office manager. We seemed to rub each other up the wrong way from the word go. The job was OK, however, and although the tasks were new, it seemed that every other job I had ever done had prepared me for this one.

It was at the college that I met George, who worked as a lecturer there. All the staff shared the same staff room, and I got to know him as he joked and talked to everyone. I learned that his wife had MS and that he had a little girl, May. Later Betty (George's wife) deteriorated and was hospitalised. The college grounds had an open air swimming pool, and in the school summer holidays the staff were allowed to use it. I said that perhaps my girls Lizzie and Jane could help keep an eye on May as George had a problem finding babysitters. Betty's condition deteriorated further and she had a blood clot in her leg which moved suddenly and she died. George was lost and shocked, and people did not know what to say to him. I was concerned that he and other people should not think I was in any way chasing after him, and kept out of his way as much as possible. After two months he said he would like to talk to me and suggested going out one evening. We went to a local pub and he spent two hours telling me all about Betty. I hardly got a word in edgeways and he just spilled out all his sadness and wanted to talk about her and her illness and death. After that we started to see each other, and he and May would sometimes come to tea on Sunday afternoon.

Then George got invited to Australia for Christmas to stay with some friends there. I was surprised how much I missed him and was pleased when he phoned me all the way from Australia. They came back to the U.K. in January, and in February he proposed to me. I was taken by surprise and not sure what to say; I initially said no because I needed time to pray and think before giving him an answer.

The saying goes 'Once bitten, twice shy' and I was going to have to be sure how to respond. No-way was I going to marry a non-Christian again. Well, I prayed and listened; after a few days I felt God was saying to me, "I have given him to you to comfort and strengthen you," and so I said yes. George had taken time to tell me that he had been to confirmation classes and had recently been confirmed just before Betty died. I think initially this had been in response to his wife's wishes, but nevertheless his commitment was real enough and he subsequently got baptised at Christ Church. Our decision to live in Bracknell was largely due to the girl's educational needs and my wish that they should complete their schooling. May was in junior school and so it was much easier to move her than the older girls who were into their GCSEs. We married in April 1983, Lizzie took her exams in the June, and the week her exams were over we moved into our new home.

The wedding was a quiet one. We talked about it beforehand with the minister and elder, and they had agreed we could marry in Christ

Church. The whole thing was very low-key and simple. A friend made some dresses for the three girls, and I bought a yellow crêpe dress off the peg with a large cream hat. I made a small reception buffet at our house and invited around twenty friends. The morning of the wedding I spent most of the time preparing the buffet and organising and helping the girls to get ready. I had literally about five minutes to get myself ready. Granny came to stay with the girls while we had a week's honeymoon in Scotland. They had written on the car with lipstick and we drove around Scotland all week with "have a lovely honeymoon from your darling daughters" written all over the vehicle as we couldn't get it off.

For our honeymoon in Scotland, George booked three different hotels for our week away. Although it was April, it was very cold, and the first morning we woke up in St John's Town of Dalrye, there was about two inches of snow on the ground. George was first to look out of the window and told me of the snow, and I said, "Pull the other leg; it's got bells on," as I didn't believe him and thought he was joking. We enjoyed the snow and walked in the woods and played snowballs. It was magical. Later on in the week, we went to Younger Botanic Garden where there were daffodils in flower. Also, at Moffat we stayed in a small hotel near a stream associated with Robbie Burns and were pleasantly surprised at the accommodation there. There were only six people staying in the hotel, and one evening they served us a whole salmon on a silver salver – very posh, and very delicious! We enjoyed Moffat, a small market town, with a little boating lake and gardens. Many years later in Madeira, we happened to get to know a couple who, it turned out, owned the baker's shop in Moffat High Street.

My full-time job at the college soon became too much once I was married. Now I was keeping house for George and three girls, plus my father. It was exhausting, and no way could I manage a full-time job as well. So I looked again for part-time work and preferably something with school holidays, as May was still young.

As I said, we moved house the day following Lizzie's GCSE exams, as I didn't want her to have to cope with the upheaval in the run-up to, or in the middle of, exams. We moved ourselves, having hired a van, and a friend helped with everything. George's house sold quickly, but selling my old home proved problematic. From our marriage in April to the end of June, both George's belongings and what was left of mine were squashed into the house. Also, of course, there were a few bits and pieces of Dad's belongings too, as he was living with me. The result was that the whole house was filled to capacity and there were boxes everywhere. Prospective buyers who came to view the house had to literally climb over boxes to get to places, and the house was crammed full. Needless to say, we did not get a buyer until we had actually moved out. In order to be able to do this, Granny very kindly loaned us some money so that we did not have to have a bridging loan from the bank. Keiran, I hasten to add, made it very plain that if we did not repay the loan at the earliest opportunity, he would sue us for the money... However, we had no intention of taking advantage of her kindness and paid the money back the minute the sale went through. Of course, Keiran then had half of the proceeds for the house.

Hindsight is a wonderful thing, and only as years passed could I see that God had taken two unhappy situations and created a new family. Amazingly, the three girls all got on well together. One hears stories of families not working out, and I'm convinced it was God's handiwork to enable our new family to knit together.

"And we know that in all things God works for the good of those who love him, who have been called according to his purpose."[4]

---

[4] Romans 8:28

CHAPTER TEN

Disney and Partnership Mission

HAVING GOT OVER MOVING HOUSE, ONCE THE OLD house was sold and finances settled, it appeared that we had a spare amount of cash. We asked the girls if they would like a special holiday now that we were a new family and where they would like to go. Of course, the answer was "Disney" – every child's dream holiday.

So the year after we married, in 1984, we took the children on a holiday to Florida. We flew to Miami and stayed our first night in Fort Lauderdale. Driving in America was frightening. On picking up the hire car, we turned out of the airport complex onto a highway full of traffic with six lanes going in each direction! It took some getting used to; thankfully, it was not far from the airport to Fort Lauderdale where we had accommodation in a motel for our first night.

We drove from there south to the Keys and then to the west coast and north to Naples, Fort Myers and east to Orlando and Cape Canaveral. Driving on the other side of the road does present its problems, as we had to get used to the different traffic signs. One evening after dark, we were returning from Cape Canaveral and managed to take a wrong turning onto a dual carriageway (or 'divided highway' as it's called). You can imagine our fear as all of a sudden we saw two sets of headlights side by side and coming straight towards us! Between the two carriageways was a stretch of grass, and George's immediate reaction was to swing the car across the central reservation to the other side. The car bounced and flew just like something out of *Starsky and Hutch,* but we landed safely on the other side. A lot of the divides between the highways in Florida have deep ditches and so we were very fortunate to have made it safely. God certainly looked after us that night. The girls said, "Please don't do that again!" – as if we would...

It was a common habit for every waitress to introduce herself and say to the customers, "Hi, I'm _____ and I'm your waitress for this evening." After a while we got pretty fed up with this constant and ingenuous patter, and so George replied, "Hi, I'm George. This is my wife, this is Lizzie, this is Jane and this is May. We are your customers for this evening." The look of surprise was obvious; she must have thought that her 'British' customers were a bit nutty.

Using motel chains was a good way to get around and quite economical as we paid for one large room that had two large queen-sized beds plus a 'roller bed' for May. Each of the motels provided a free phone service so that you could book ahead each day from one place to the next. Apart from the driving debacle, Cape Canaveral was a fascinating place to see with all the spaceships and paraphernalia.

Disney, of course, was the highlight of the trip, and we spent two days visiting the Magic Kingdom and one day in Epcot. We stayed late one evening and saw the magical Electrical Parade with illuminated floats and Disney characters. We thought at the time it was a 'once in a lifetime' trip; little did we think then we would be coming back to the U.S. many times.

The next time we went to U.S. was with the Partnership Mission organisation led by Rev. Jim White. The scheme was that churches in America and the U.K. exchanged teams of people who would help with a week's mission.

George and I felt that it was right for us to volunteer. Because we thought it was what God wanted us to do, we committed to paying our air fare, which was quite a lot of money then, and it was quite remarkable the way that God honoured our decision to go regardless of the fact that it would take our family holiday money. What happened next was amazing, as our trip was paid for.

The story behind this incredible provision begins way back during the Second World War... My mother befriended an injured serviceman called Ron who was convalescing in Oxford. He had a severe head wound and never worked again. He remained friends with us after the war and throughout my childhood came to visit us from Leamington Spa. He used to bring us a dozen freshly laid eggs, which was a great treat in the years of rationing after the war. Ron was a quiet gentleman who never married and, faced with old age and going into a home, decided to send gifts to all the people who had helped him over the years. By this time, my mother had died some years before and so he sent that gift to me.

It was the very same day that our payment for the trip to America was due that Ron's cheque came through our letterbox. Amazed, George picked up the letter and said, "Guess what? Our travel to Florida is provided for." God is so gracious; if I had had any misgivings and worries about going to America on the mission, they were instantly gone. I now knew for sure that we were doing the right thing.

We joined a group of about a couple of dozen people and travelled to Orlando. There we were divided up into smaller groups of five or six and assigned a local church. We went to Pinecastle Church and stayed in some accommodation belonging to the owner of a ski boats company.

We stayed in the company apartment, which was comfortable, if old-fashioned. The standing joke was that it had a bowl of plastic fruit on the table which George called "plasticus domesticus".

The kindly gentleman who was the head of the family business told us his story. Following Pearl Harbour, his company was instructed to build boats for the American war effort and told to work seven days a week. He refused, saying he and his staff would not work on a Sunday. He claimed that his company would turn out more boats in six days than those who worked every day. He kept his word and his company met all the quotas required. His boats were top class and he was made chairman of the local Board of Commerce. He told us how he used to begin all his meetings for the board with prayer. His boats were used in various attractions, and he arranged for our group to pay a visit to Global Marine and see the International Team of Christian Water Skiers that he helped sponsor.

It was usual for the church activities to centre around some kind of food – it could be breakfast at the local diner, or lunch, or a 'pot luck supper' to which everyone brought something and it was just pot luck that it didn't turn out to be forty salads or forty desserts. Several of the families of the church invited us to their homes for meals, and it was amusing that they made the assumption that because we were English we would like trifle. I think that almost everywhere we went we were offered trifle because our kindly hosts thought that was what the Brits ate. As well as church services, during the week of mission we joined in all the neighbourhood activities with Pinecastle Church. The church was involved in serving the community in many ways: a literacy group for immigrants from Puerto Rico; a daily lunch club for the elderly called the 'Live Long and Like It Club'; delivering lunches to poor people; visiting housebound people. One such man had posters and stickers for wallpaper – a very different view of Florida to what tourists see (he reminded me of Onslow in *Keeping Up Appearances*). Out and about, just going to the supermarket, it was amazing how many opportunities there were for witnessing. "You Brits talk funny – why are you here?" was the common opening.

One particular event sticks in my mind, as God really blessed me through it. A few of us visited a home where elderly and sick people were being cared for. We led a short service with songs and a message and then circulated to talk to the people there. As I mingled among the inmates, a lady came up to me and began to cry. Her cries became more and more distressing, and she wailed aloud and was very upset. I sat her down and tried to talk to her, but she was becoming hysterical. I managed to get her to tell me what was the matter. She said that she had a brain tumour and was dying and she was really scared. She didn't know if she would go to heaven or hell; she was so frightened and no-one would talk to her. What an opportunity – we did talk and I was able to share the gospel with her. Finally, we prayed together for her to receive Christ and his forgiveness. When I left her, she was quiet and calm and altogether different.

It was not until later that evening that I was thinking about the events of the day and wondering why, out of all the people in that room, she singled me out. I thanked God for being able to talk to her and for the difference I had seen in her as she accepted the Lord Jesus. Then, as I wrote my diary of the day, it was as if a light suddenly came on. A revelation! God had allowed me the privilege of ministering to that lady as part of His purpose to save her and bless her, but also to bless me – He knew that I felt very guilty about not talking to my sister Phyllis who had also died of a brain tumour, to enable her to voice her fears and receive comfort and peace from God. So in his mercy and grace, He gave me a second chance to do just that...

CHAPTER ELEVEN

A New Routine and New Happenings

AND SO IT WAS THAT LIFE SETTLED AGAIN INTO A NEW routine. Now that I had George, three girls, my father and two pets to look after, it became too much to cope with full-time working. I soon moved on from the Three Counties College to work at the social services department. Strangely, I moved back into the original building where the art school used to be, but which was now social services. I worked part-time as secretary for two of the directors there.

The women with whom I worked and shared an office were very friendly, and after a while some of us agreed to meet together in the staff room during our lunch break so that we could learn bridge. Bridge is a strategic card game, and I had always been keen on playing cards, having done so for years with the family, albeit simple family games. Ruby agreed to teach us, and so three of us joined her so that we could learn. Over the years it has become a source of fun and also a challenge to be a good player. It has also become a mission field, opening up the world of bridge clubs and widening my circle of friends and acquaintances. As we became more proficient, we had occasion to go away on a 'Bridge Weekend' to a hotel in Bournemouth. A typical bridge weekend would include games on Friday evening, some teaching on Saturday morning and playing again on Saturday evening. During some free time on the Saturday afternoon, I was out walking along Boscombe cliffs with Ruby, and she expressed a desire to know more about my faith. I was able to talk to her about how I became a Christian, and she said she would very much like to do the same. On returning home, she began to attend her local church and is now a lovely Christian and still a dear friend.

Lizzie was by now doing 'A' levels and studying hard. Jane began her GCSEs and May was settled in the juniors. The most frequent comment from the teachers at May's school was "talks too much", and I guess she mostly took after her dad.

We had some fun times together. We went to a holiday camp at Christchurch. May went in for a dancing competition and won – she was very proud. We have albums of holidays, and life consisted mainly of work (school or other), occasional holidays and church. Each of the girls had their own friendships, and we enjoyed seeing their various friends. As they got older and boyfriends appeared on the scene, George had an unusual strategy to deter the young boys he didn't take to. When they visited the house, he would call them 'Malcolm' regardless of their actual name. You can imagine it was a bit off-putting as the conversation progressed and still he spoke to them calling them 'Malcolm'. But the funniest thing was one day when the tables were turned – Jane brought a young man home and introduced him, and he really was called Malcolm. As the older ones left home, we had a couple of holidays where we took one or other of May's friends with us for company. We had some Easter holidays at an event called 'Spring Harvest' (usually held at the Butlin's holiday camps) and May and her friend cajoled George continually all through the week to go on the loop-the-loop fair ride that was part of the funfair at the camp in Ayr. These Christian holidays were great fun for the girls, because there were lots of events for teenagers and for us too. I was grateful the girls were happy in coming to church, and I was 'over the moon' when one by one they made their own commitments to Christ and were baptised.

As well as his work at the college, George also had a few friends whom he helped by doing some gardening at weekends. Henry was one such, and he and Elaine lived in north Bracknell; George regularly visited to prune things and give them advice about the garden. This went on for some time, and then Henry became ill. It transpired he had cancer and eventually was pronounced terminal. He had his bed downstairs, and George obviously had been witnessing to him because he asked if I would go to see him and pray for him. I didn't know Henry, and as I cycled the short distance to his home, I prayed for God to help me and show me how to talk to him. On arriving, I was shown into his room and sat at the end of his bed. He looked at me strangely and said, "Why have you come to see me looking like that?" "What do you mean?" I asked. He said, "You've got rags on; why have you come to see me dressed like that?" I was amazed; *he thinks I'm dressed in rags! What's going on?*

Then I realised God had supernaturally caused him to see me that way and that was my clue as to how to talk to him. You see, Henry had led a very good and upright life and, as far as he was concerned, he didn't think he needed a Saviour. He needed to know how without Jesus he was still a sinner and that his 'good life' would not enable him to be acceptable to God. Scripture says, "All our righteous acts are like filthy rags,"[5] and, "...all have sinned and fall short of the glory of God..."[6] Henry responded positively as I explained this to him, and he received Christ for himself. How wonderful, what a privilege, to see God at work like that and be a part of it.

After Henry died, his wife moved away from Bracknell to live near family on the south coast. We continued to visit her, and she would make us very welcome, but sadly, she did not have any faith herself nor any desire either.

Another person constantly in touch with us at that time was an elderly single lady from the church, who lived near our local shops. As she had no family and lived alone, we looked out for her, and she joined us for Christmas and occasional meals. Ethel certainly liked her food! She had led a sheltered life, spending the best years of her life looking after her ailing mother. She had suffered from depression and attended the local mental health clinic for some time. She was timid and a gentle soul but also good for a laugh, and George sometimes joked with her and pulled her leg. She had been attending church since her childhood, but on talking to her, I realised her Bible understanding was very limited, and so we agreed to do some studies together so that I could explain to her in very simple terms the truths of the gospel. As we looked at the Bible together, it became apparent that most of the teaching at church had gone straight over her head, and Ethel grew in her faith at last.

---

[5] Isaiah 64:6
[6] Romans 3:23

Our first few years of marriage were good – busy but good. As time went on, however, it became apparent that George was suffering from stress. Things became tricky and I found myself being a 'piggy in the middle', always mediating between him and the girls. Around the time Lizzie finished her 'A' levels and left school, she had three months to fill before starting college in the autumn. I went to an elder at the church and asked him if he knew of anywhere that Lizzie and her friend Janice could go to work for the summer. He was so helpful and arranged for a friend of his who owned a hotel on the Isle of Wight to engage both Lizzie and her school friend Janice for the summer season, and so I was very relieved for Lizzie to spend the summer there. That way she also was able to save some money towards her living expenses at college in the autumn.

That summer sticks in my mind because Jane, May, George and I spent our holiday in an old caravan in Swanage. It was dreadful, really old and wheels rusted into the grass. The reason we ended up there was because we had not booked in advance; there was no other accommodation. This caravan was all that was available, and no wonder. There was an outside loo; to get to this you had to pass by a goat tethered to a post. It rained and rained, and in two weeks we clocked up just six hours of sunshine. After that experience, I vowed to go abroad even if it meant only having a holiday every two or three years. We spent one day on Brownsea Island, and the drizzle became steady rain and we got soaked – even more so when a passing boat swamped us with still more water. Jane and May made the best of it – bless them – and even said that the holiday was good because, on returning to school, they had lots to write about as we had spent the two weeks visiting every attraction there was and going from one place to the next trying to avoid the bad weather.

Lizzie left home and went to Nottingham School of Physiotherapy. Two years later Jane got her 'A' levels and went to Exeter University. My babies were leaving the nest. I was glad for them and prayed hard for God to keep them safe. He did.

Last of all, May went to live in London in the nurses' hostel at Great Ormond Street Hospital. Of the three, hers was the most final moving out, as she only came home for one weekend after that, preferring to stay with her fiancé's family. We were so proud each time one of our girls made their way into the big world and even more proud as they got their diplomas.

Despite George's tactics designed to deter the boys, the three girls met their future husbands, and we were thrilled to see them all happily married. Some of my sewing skills came in handy, as I was able to make the bridesmaids' dresses. Their weddings were such happy occasions.

How blessed I have been – I tell my friends I have been more blessed than the Queen to see my girls become Christians, have Christian husbands and have lasting marriages.

CHAPTER TWELVE

America, America

IT WAS IN 1988 THAT WE FIRST WENT TO VISIT BRUCE AND his wife Joyce, who lived in Kansas, U.S.

George had shared an office at the Three Counties College with Bruce, who came to the U.K. for a year on a teacher's exchange. Bruce's first wife Barbara died and he remarried to Joyce in Kansas. Joyce and Bruce lived in a mobile home on a small-holding-cum-farm belonging to Joyce's son. They had so much land – for us living in the U.K. where land is a premium, their land just seemed to go on and on forever. When you stood outside their mobile home and looked around to the horizon in every direction, it was all their land. Our visit was in the summer holidays because of the difficulty of taking May out of school, and it was very hot.

En route we stopped off at New York for three days. We had to change flights there anyway and I didn't want to miss the opportunity of seeing something of the city that I had heard a lot about. I asked Jim White if he knew of any pastors in Manhattan who would be willing to help us. He put us in touch with a pastor to whom I wrote, and he passed my letter to another pastor on Manhattan Island. We stayed in a reasonably priced hotel in Times Square for a few nights, and this pastor and his wife took us round and showed us the sights for three days. He had an amazing testimony as he used to be a model and also a drug addict, and now he was pastoring a street church in New York and working with some of the drug addicts there. He and his wife and two little boys lived in a very small apartment in Manhattan. They invited us for a meal one evening, and we were amazed to see that their apartment consisted of one living room with a very small kitchenette, a landing and one small bedroom and bathroom. Their two little boys had the bedroom, and they slept on the landing. It was very expensive to rent an apartment in Manhattan, and they considered it amazing they could live there at all. Because there was a high level of crime in New York, they advised us not to look too much like tourists and not to go out after dark except in a taxi. We spent a couple of very happy and exhausting days walking all around downtown with them and the boys in a pushchair, camera to the ready.

Next door to our hotel in Times Square was a delicatessen. We stopped there briefly to buy some bottled water to drink during our daily walkabout. When I asked the man behind the counter if I could have some water, he looked at me in a puzzled fashion and then said, "We don't have tha-a-at," in his American drawl. I repeated that I wanted to buy some *water*, speaking more slowly as I thought he possibly didn't understand because of my English accent. "We don't have tha-a-at," he said again. "Got some *wadder*?" says George, and, "Oh, we have tha-a-at," he said laughing at us. We walked out of the deli and the two shop assistants looked at each other and repeated "Waa-t-er, waa-t-er" to each other.

Because it was August and New York was very hot, a lot of the pastor's 'flock' were away, so they had some spare time. We appreciated their help very much, especially when he took us on the underground to catch the first boat across to Liberty Island so that we could go up the Statue of Liberty. Even at that time of day, early in the morning, the underground was *very* hot and stifling. As we approached the entrance, he told us to brace ourselves for the extreme heat. We caught the first boat of the day over to Liberty Island at 8 am. The Statue of Liberty is hollow and made of metal, and we walked up the very cramped spiral stairs to the crown, which was also the viewing platform. What an amazing view! By the time we came down, it was already very hot even though it was only 10 am, and the inside and exterior of the statue was too hot to touch. We were so thankful to have had his help to do the trip early in the day. Some years later we heard he had died of cancer, and later still we were glad to hear that his widow had remarried. Ours was a brief friendship yet another illustration of God's provision for our every need and such a blessing.

Following our brief stopover in New York, we continued our journey to Kansas. When we got off the plane in Kansas, it was about four o'clock in the afternoon and cooling down, and yet it was still a hundred and four Fahrenheit. Whilst staying with Bruce and Joyce, we would get up early, and then by 11 am it was too hot to do anything so we went indoors. After about 4 pm, it cooled down sufficiently to be able to go outside again. We sat outdoors in the evening and watched the fireflies and electric storms all around us. We drank iced tea which Joyce prepared by putting a jug of cold water with a tea bag on the porch to steep all day in the sun. Later she added ice and we were supposed to drink it, but I didn't like it much. Give me a good cup of hot tea any day! The Americans think we Brits are mad drinking hot tea in the hot weather.

Bruce and Joyce took us on a trip to Colorado and we visited their daughter in Colorado Springs. We drove through the rocky mountains to Mesa Verde, where Indians used to live in caves. Bruce's sayings still echo in our minds: "Burger King Joyce" – Burger King was one of Bruce's favourite places to eat, and when faced with puzzling directions before the days of satnavs, he used to say, "Joyce you can't get there from here." Dairy Queen was another favourite place for ice creams / dessert, although Bruce and Joyce used to make their own strawberry ice cream by the gallon. One eventful day on our trip to Colorado was a visit to Pikes Peak, which is fourteen thousand feet above sea level. We drove to the top with Bruce and Joyce and were amazed that it was very cold and the air was thin at the top. It was a lovely clear, sunny day and so the view was amazing. On the way down, a park ranger halted us to inspect the brakes on the car, because they were likely to overheat. We were told to take a break and wait for the brakes to cool off, so we left the car for a short while and sat overlooking the lovely view and admiring the little chipmunks that abounded there.

In that part of the Rockies we also visited Durango and Silverton, towns famous from the old 'goldrush' days. An old original steam train straight out of the westerns still runs from Durango to Silverton, but we could not ride on it because it was fully booked about a year ahead. We did go to an interesting restaurant to eat, where we had very hot fajitas. Because of the close proximity to Mexico, a lot of the food there was very spicy. Years later we still remember a waitress asking us if we wanted "Ra-a-a-a-an-n-n-nch Sa-a-a-auce" in her southern American drawl. We found her accent amusing, as no doubt she did ours.

Bruce died of cancer some years later, but we managed to see them a few times. Joyce outlived him but ended up with dementia and was cared for by her many children.

Before they became too elderly, they used to like going on 'Elder Hostel' holidays. It was on one of these holidays that Bruce and Joyce met Eileen and Jim who, according to Bruce, talked just like us – meaning that they were Christians and were enthusiastic about God.

Eileen and Jim were coming to the U.K. for a week's mission in the Bristol area (a bit like the Partnership Mission trip we had in Orlando) and they had planned to visit London for a couple of days once the mission was finished. Bruce and Joyce asked us if we would put them up for a couple of nights. We did so, and immediately we struck a chord together. They did indeed visit London, and we also took them to Windsor and to see local sights. By the end of our few days together, we had become firm friends, and being the hospitable people they were, they invited us back to visit them in Wisconsin.

And so we journeyed to Wisconsin – first to Milwaukee and then with Eileen and Jim to Waupaca on the chain of lakes. Jim worked for a company in Chicago, and they lived in a pleasant residential part of Milwaukee. Eileen took us to see the Milwaukee domes, which were large bio domes similar to the Eden Project in Cornwall. Of course, these were operational long before the ones in Cornwall were built. We also went to see the tallest building in Milwaukee, which was a hundred and four floors high. We went up in the lift, but George surprised us by saying that he didn't want to go down in the lift, he wanted to walk down. So we came down in the lift and then sat at the bottom for fifteen minutes whilst George walked down over a hundred flights of stairs! After that, Eileen always referred to that building as 'George's building'.

Eileen and Jim and their family were all Christians, and they too had an amazing testimony of how God had rescued them from alcoholism. In particular, one of their children had had a serious problem with alcohol and he too had completed changed since he became a Christian. They lived simply, and both Eileen and Jim were into fitness and healthy eating in a big way. Jim ran several miles every couple of days, and Eileen did speed walking. She would bake bran muffins, and they ate home-popped corn with salt and no butter. They were both fit and active, and enjoyed showing us their beautiful country.

The most beautiful place was at Waupaca, where there was a chain of lakes. They had a large house (which they called a cottage) near one of the lakes. It was idyllic and so beautiful. We visited with their friends and their church, and they took us around to places like Madison and the House on the Rock, Wisconsin Dells and to the historical district and Door County. Eileen was just the sweetest person and the most Christ-like person I've ever met. In many ways, I felt like she was a sister to me, appreciating her love, because I missed having that sort of relationship with my own blood sister, Beryl.

Eileen and Jim visited us again in the U.K., and we also visited them in Florida where they lived at the D & D Missionary homes. Because of the cold winters in Wisconsin, it was common for people to move to Florida for the winter months. Eileen and Jim worked as volunteers at the D&D homes, where missionaries who had come home from serving overseas were kitted out and equipped with everything they would need for living in the U.S. Eventually, Eileen too died of cancer – we made a special trip to see her before she died; she was such a precious friend. Jim married again, but somehow we couldn't bring ourselves to visit them again without Eileen being there. And so, without our dear friends, our visits to the US came to an end.

During our visits, however, we also got to know Henry and Arlene, who some years later rang us out of the blue and asked us if we could accommodate a young girl called Bonny who was studying to be an architect. Apparently, she wanted to learn about English architecture and wanted to live in the U.K. She lived with us for a few months whilst she looked for a job here. She managed to get a job in Thame and left us to live in Oxford. She went to a local church there and met a young man whom she married. Unfortunately, the marriage did not work out and very quickly Bonny went back to America to her family. Ten years later she returned to England and married another young man whom she had also met in Oxford and with whom she had been corresponding. To cut a long story short, she and her family of three boys are now living in the U.S. again, and we are pleased to still be in touch and hear their news from time to time.

CHAPTER THIRTEEN

Depression – A Different World

MY WORK AT SOCIAL SERVICES CAME TO AN END DUE TO a restructuring, whereby in order to keep my current job, I would have to travel to the East Berks office each day. It was some miles away and there was no mention of compensation for extra time and cost of travel. I was unsure of what was best to do and so prayed and asked God. I also shared my problem with the house group to which we belonged and asked them to pray for me as well. The outcome was that I decided it was time for me to leave. I didn't know what would happen in the future but felt it was right to finish working there. They were surprised and said there would be no redundancy payout as I had been offered another job, but no – I had made the decision.

The restructuring eventually happened in the September, and from then until Christmas I had some months of rest, doing some household jobs that I never got round to and, most importantly, having some quality times with God. Christmas was enjoyable as usual, and then early in the new year George suffered a mental breakdown.

The crux of the problem was that George had a new boss at the college where he worked – a woman who was making his life very difficult. The college had changed from being run by the county council to a private limited company and, as such, had now to generate its own income. As a result, they were running all sorts of different courses, some of which George was required to teach regardless of whether he had the knowledge to do so. He had been under a lot of pressure and finally cracked. He had his Christmas 1992 break but when it was time to go back to work in January, he couldn't cope. His breakdown resulted in a depression that lasted over two years. A desperate attempt to get back to work in March 1993 only resulted in him becoming worse.

During that first year he was in and out of General Park Psychiatric Hospital three times, each time staying for a month. In my ignorance and optimism I thought that going into hospital would result in change and healing. At that time I was also convinced that God would heal him quickly – I was wrong about that too.

All that resulted was that they gave him pills and more pills. Most of the time he was very anxious and sad; he cried a great deal and wanted me to be with him all the time, even to the point of being in the same room. I found it hard, not only to cope with the constant replaying record that said "I'll never go back to work", but with the constant drain on my resources. It seemed like the more sympathetic I was, the more he would soak it up like a sponge and drain me. I had to address this and become 'tougher' in order to keep my own sanity.

The pills made him very dopey, and I used to have to work hard at getting him up in the morning. I would literally make him dress and say, "Come on, we're going out." We would go for walks – anywhere – just to get out. He wanted me there all the time, and I found this very wearing. I needed some space. Our church house group met in the evenings and I decided to go on one occasion, but was summoned home again. On another occasion, in sheer desperation, I called on Lizzie and Daniel. Lizzie came and talked to me whilst Daniel talked to George – things got very bad.

The doctors said he would never recover sufficiently to do without his medication. From time to time, as it appeared that his medication was not working enough, he would be changed onto something different. This in itself presented problems, because going from one set of pills to another meant that during the three-week time slot in getting used to them, he was actually worse. He was assigned a community psychiatric nurse, who was very helpful and gave us support when we needed it. It was a relief to have someone I could phone if George got bad spells – and some of them were *very* bad when he wanted to self-harm and talked of suicide. It was on these occasions that he was admitted to hospital for his own protection.

As time went by, he started attending a day centre for the mentally ill in Bracknell, which incidentally was the centre that Ethel had attended years before. This was a good stepping stone, and he got used to going there a couple of days a week. This helped me too as it gave me a break and some space for myself. Many of the people at the centre had been going there for years. They did various activities including art, and George produced several pictures. I learned later on that artwork can be very therapeutic for people to express their inmost thoughts and feelings.

Friends at Christ Church were kind and supportive, although no-one really knew just how things were for us. But they tried, and showed us love, which was the most important thing. They encouraged George to keep attending church, although he found this difficult. He found it virtually impossible to read the Bible and pray because he totally lost his concentration. He did, however, remember the 23rd Psalm and was able to keep looking at that. The pastor and his wife supported me, as no-one seemed able to help George at that time. I used to see them for an hour once a month to talk about how things had been and to pray. I know others in the church were praying for us, and it was a comfort to know this, even though at the time we were not seeing answers.

God seemed far away for both of us for a long time, and my faith reached its lowest ebb. I began questioning whether God was really both loving and all-powerful. If He was all-powerful and yet was not answering our prayers, how could He be good and loving, allowing this to continue? If, on the other hand, He was not able to heal George then He was not all-powerful. I got very confused, and unbelief started gaining ground. I did try to pray, but the prayers felt very ineffective; it felt like I was hitting a brick wall. The depression dragged on, and it seemed like it would go on forever – there was no light at the end of the tunnel. I was getting on dangerous ground, almost to a place of turning my back on God.

Then I went to a special meeting organised by several of the local churches. I don't remember anything about the theme or talk, but what did speak to me was a comment made by the speaker towards the end of the evening when he stated that someone there was very close to walking away from God and He wanted them to know what a crucial time this was and to come back. I just knew in my spirit that message was for me and I was sorry for my unbelief; I thanked God for holding on to me when I found it so difficult to hold on to Him.

I still found it hard to pray, and often sat and cried instead of praying. One day God spoke to me through Job 16:19-21: "Even now my witness is in heaven; my advocate is on high. My intercessor is my friend as my eyes pour out tears to God; On behalf of a man he pleads with God as one pleads for a friend." *Who is my intercessor,* I asked myself. Romans 8:34 came to mind: "Christ Jesus who died – more than that, who was raised to life – is at the right hand of God and is also interceding for us." I knew then Jesus was interceding for me, He was my advocate, and even if all I could do was cry, then God still heard and knew. That glimmer of light encouraged me to carry on.

After some time had gone by, one day I did hear from God and knew that he would heal George. I was reading 1 Thessalonians 4:11: "Make it your ambition to lead a quiet life, you should mind your own business and work with your hands, just as we told you, so that your daily life may win the respect of outsiders and so that you will not be dependent on anybody."

The words jumped off the page at me – *George will work with his hands.*

"OK," I said, "George will work with his hands." Then the penny dropped: *if he is going to work with his hands, then he is going to get better* (at that moment in time he was not fit to do anything).

I knew then in that moment he would be healed and from then on could pray with faith for his healing. I knew it was going to happen. He took an early retirement from his job and seemed reassured in the knowledge that he would not have to return. The doctors were still saying he would never get off his medication and would need it for the rest of his life. In some kind of topsy-turvy way, that statement activated his stubborn streak and helped to goad him into wanting to do the opposite and come off his medication.

Learning to be patient and waiting for God to act is hard and not necessarily a pleasant experience. I needed to learn to trust God. I have often said I am trusting God, but is that true and am I waiting in a positive frame of mind? I certainly had many lessons to learn, as well as George's situation; there were other lengthy years of waiting for my grandchildren to be born.

Both Lizzie and Jane had to wait several years for their babies. Eventually, they were in their thirties when our prayers were answered. I knew God had told me that He would bless my children's children, and yet both my daughters were struggling to conceive. I kept praying and standing on his word. Eventually, Lizzie and Daniel came to see us one day and during the conversation asked what we would be doing the following spring. What a strange question, how would I know – that was more than six months away. "We'll be needing a babysitter," Lizzie said. What joy – and how we both cried with happiness. Jane too was waiting similarly, and in her sisterly love also praying she would not conceive before her sister, knowing just how hard that would be for her. And so Jane also followed just a few months after Lizzie. What timing; God is good!

During protracted difficult times when we know that those dear to us are suffering, it is not easy to keep on praying with faith. "Keep on keeping on," an old friend of mine used to say. God wants me to learn to walk by faith rather than focussing on my feelings. Hindsight is a wonderful thing; now, looking back, I can see how God was working.

CHAPTER FOURTEEN

Road to Recovery

HOW SLOWLY THIS PROCESS WENT ON, BUT JUST AS IT HAD taken years to bring him to the point of the breakdown, so it took years to take the steps to recovery. It is easy to slide down a slippery slope, but hard and slow to take the steps back up again.

A catalyst came in the form of a visit to the consultant at the hospital. It was one of several regular visits to monitor his progress, and on this occasion the doctor was emphatic that George would need medication for the rest of his life. George was upset by this prognosis and decided he would prove the doctor wrong. He said he was going to try to get off his medication. I was aware of the very real danger of just coming off and precipitating a relapse, so we agreed to reduce the number of tablets he was taking very, *very* slowly over a long period of several months. Little by little and ever so slowly began the transition of reducing his dependency on medication. Eventually, after a long time, he saw his local GP for a routine visit and told him what he had been doing. When the GP found out the amount of medication he was actually taking, he said he might as well stop since the dose was now so small as to be ineffective anyway.

Following negotiations with his employer and anticipating George's half-pension starting in April 1994, I decided it was time for me to go back to work. Our income would be considerably reduced, and not only did we need the money, I needed the space to get out of the house sometimes too. In November 1993 I applied for a part-time job at a youth centre. At the time of my application, I was stretched between visiting Ken, my brother-in-law, in Oxford who had cancer and looking after George, and I literally had ten minutes to fill in the form by hand. I pushed it through the letterbox of the building that evening because there was no time to post it, the deadline for applications being the following morning. I didn't think I could be offered the job on such a scrappy application but, amazingly, I was, and I started work at the youth centre in January 1994. At the prospect of my being out of the house, George immediately reacted with more anxiety, and I knew that I had to be strong and just stick to my guns and do it. Ken died on the day before my fiftieth birthday in December 1993. All in all, 1993 was such a tough year; I was glad when it ended.

In the autumn of 1994 George saw an advert in the paper for a gardener for sixteen hours a week. He said he would like to try and do it, but anxiety reared its ugly head again and it took him a whole week to pluck up the courage to ring up and enquire about it. Of course, by the time he actually phoned, the job was already taken. He took that as an indication that he was not ready yet to try to work again and decided to leave it for a while. The following spring we were surprised to get a phone call from the couple who had placed the advert, saying that the gardener had left and would George like to visit them with a view to applying for a job? It seemed that of all the people who had phoned about the previous vacancy – surprise, surprise! – George's was the only phone number they had kept! George went to talk to them and it turned out that they too were Christians. They were very kind to George, who told them all about his experience at the college and his subsequent illness. He told them that he was worried about taking the step to try to get back to work because he would lose all his state benefits, and if it didn't work out then we would have to go all through the process again to get them back.

They went out of their way to help us. George was told he could go and help in the garden for as long as he liked, and each day when he felt that he had had enough, he could just simply go home. There was no pressure; he could come and go as he pleased. We agreed that he would not be paid until he was happy that he could cope and would be able to come off benefits. The rules for receiving benefits were such that he could not work more than sixteen hours a week. And so George started, very tentatively, back to work unpaid. He was so anxious and fearful, but little by little he gained in confidence. After he had been going regularly for several months, he said that he felt that he could take the step to come off benefits. During this time he had not received any wages but had still been drawing his benefits. So in the summer of 1995 he made the transition back to work – something he was convinced would never happen, but God gives us "immeasurably more than all we ask or imagine"[7] and the lovely couple gave George a gift to help compensate him for his months of working for nothing. We were amazed and so grateful. I remembered God's word to me from months before that he would "work with his hands". Thank You, Lord; You healed him in the end and we learned a lot of lessons along the way.

Following this, an old student of George's, a lady called Caroline, contacted him. She had heard of his illness and wanted to help. She lived in a small village and said that a small group of her friends would like him to come and talk to them about plants. He said, "No way! I can't do it," but she eventually persuaded him to go with the assurance that it would be very low-key and only a very few people would be there. He reluctantly and tentatively agreed that he would do half a dozen short talks over a six-month period. When it came to the first one, George prepared for two whole days, going over his old notes and sorting out slides of plants. He was so nervous and fearful, and had very little confidence.

But he did it! The next time was the same, only not quite as bad. The subsequent times gradually improved, and by the time he had completed the six sessions, he had gained a lot of confidence again. Of course, the feeling that he had forgotten all his plant knowledge was only a symptom of the illness, and once he started doing it again, he realised that actually all his knowledge was still there after all. In fact, he has a photographic memory when it comes to plant names and has an amazing amount of knowledge. So he got back into doing talks for gardening societies locally and very gradually took up the reins of offering occasional talks about plants. Of course, we had to get permission from his teacher's pension people, but neither of his activities precluded him from continuing to receive his pension.

---

[7] Ephesians 3:20

George has given evening talks to lots of gardening clubs until recently and continued working until his retirement. I also retired from my job at the youth centre at the age of sixty-three.

God has been good and fulfilled his promise of healing. He has also provided for all our needs.

As I write this, I am mindful that now, all these years later, George is still well and at the age of seventy-four has never had a recurrence of his mental illness. He does suffer from osteoarthritis due to so many years of physical work gardening, but this does not prevent him from pottering around and enjoying his own garden. He is a never-ending fount of knowledge about plants and keen to share his enthusiasm with other people interested in their gardens. Even this year, during our Covid-constrained summer, he was keen to open his garden for visitors to raise money for charity and has begun giving talks again using Zoom.

Chapter Fifteen

The Youth Centre

I WORKED TWENTY HOURS A WEEK AT THE YOUTH centre. The building was a small, single-storey building with a tarmac flat roof. It roasted in the summer and froze in the winter. I worked there for thirteen years until my retirement.

The team consisted of around a dozen workers, mostly female, whose remit was helping families and young people. The team was multi-agency and the staff reflected the different skills needed to help teenagers. The manager was a nice person, and it was a very friendly place to be where everyone got on well together. I was the only admin support and was very busy covering all the usual office functions, including keeping the accounts and budget monitoring. I was the only Christian in the team, and it was considerate of them when I think that they avoided swearing when I was in the office. They also assumed quite correctly that I would not be joining the lottery syndicate. Nevertheless we got on well, and there were some very good and dedicated people in the team.

It's strange reviewing my time there – the funny things that stick in your memory. Ever since I was young, we have marked April Fool's Day in the family with silly jokes played on one another, and I remember a couple of such times at the youth centre. It was customary to have a team meeting once a week where everyone was present and all sorts of topics were discussed. I produced an official-looking document which I submitted to the team meeting outlining how the cigarette breaks should now be logged, enabling calculation of the day's working hours. What consternation that caused and heated discussion! Eventually, I drew their attention to the code at the bottom of the page – labelled AF1 – short for April Fool 1. A bit 'tongue in cheek', some might say. On another occasion I set up a worker who always arrived late at around 10 am. I had received the delivery of a large cardboard box addressed to her and I wrote upon it with a large felt tip pen "Light Sensitive – Open in the Dark". On her arrival she took the large box to her room and, I found out later, closed the curtains and got underneath the desk to open it! Needless to say, we used to get on well and we had a good laugh about it.

In my opinion it was a sad day when, in April 2000, the Government of the day set up 'Youth Offending Teams' and our team disbanded. Several people were redeployed in other social services offices, and those remaining were locked into working with youngsters falling foul of the police and courts. The Government wanted reporting on everything the team did – no longer was it sufficient to be a trained professional who was able to use their own initiative and set up imaginative programmes for the children; everything had to be recorded on computers and the right boxes ticked religiously. Quarterly returns became standard practice in order to assess how well the team was performing and what place that earned them on the published league tables. Where have the days of integrity and conscientious application to doing a good job gone?

My job changed and became one of statistical reporting, the main task being producing the quarterly reports. It felt to me like the world and his wife all wanted figures and percentages of who was doing what and how and when, and I was working intensively to cope with the increased demands despite my twenty allotted hours. To be fair, I was encouraged to increase my hours to full-time working, but this was something I did not wish to do. My philosophy over the years has been, do I live to work or work to live? So long as I can earn enough to live simply, then I have tended to use my time doing a variety of things rather than being locked into full-time working. I know I have been very blessed to be able to make this choice, and this was an enormous privilege as many people do not have that luxury and have to work very long hours to make ends meet.

It is said that the only certain thing in life is change. I was so glad to retire – over the thirteen years I worked there, things had changed so much and, in my opinion, not for the better. It was sad that my experience working with the team began so well and happily and ended less affably, mainly due to changes in the leadership and the emphasis of the team. Nevertheless God used that time in an unexpected way through one of the workers who one day suggested to me that I would make a good counsellor and told me to pursue this...

CHAPTER SIXTEEN

Counselling – A New Direction

IT WAS DURING THE EARLIER YEARS AT THE YOUTH centre that one of the staff did a very strange thing. We had a lady social worker who was Scandinavian and she liked to interact with the young people and build a relationship with them by taking them out on little treats. She would often take the youngsters to have a coffee in the town, or they would engage in some activity together. I was in my office as usual one day, when she came in and took a phone call to a counselling team organiser. She spoke on the phone for a few minutes, then all of a sudden said to me, "You would be good at this. Here," and thrust the phone into my hand. I spoke to the organiser, who told me that if I would like to volunteer as a helper, I could go to the counselling centre and meet with her. I subsequently did, and she was a pleasant lady who encouraged me to go along to a training course that she was running. So I joined the basic training course which ran for about twelve weeks, one evening per week. I was amazed at the simplicity and yet good sense of all that was said, and the exercises were very helpful. At the end of the course, I was told that they considered that I would be suitable to be a volunteer counsellor and asked what day and time I could contribute.

The centre was open Monday to Friday in the evenings and also on a Saturday morning. I opted to do a Saturday morning, mainly because this seemed to be a difficult slot for them to cover. It was quite nerve-wracking to start with, as I could be presented with any problem imaginable by the people who came to the centre. The set-up was that each counsellor would see their client over six visits and then consider whether another six visits would be beneficial. It was a new experience that was very rewarding when I could be of help, but also I was greatly concerned that I should be doing and saying the right thing. I was very aware of the danger of saying or doing the wrong thing that could actually make the situation worse.

One of the conditions of being a counsellor at the centre was that we should attend 'Supervision' sessions every four to six weeks. This meant attending a small group on an evening when a handful of counsellors would meet together with an experienced person who could give us advice and guide us in our efforts to be of help to our clients. These sessions were very helpful in giving each of us time to share our concerns, while at the same time respecting our clients' confidentiality, and the group having often some insightful ideas to help.

As I continued, I found the experience less scary and gradually gained confidence. I decided to undertake a training course in Counselling Skills and obtained the SE Regional Certificate. The course was for two years, after which time I would be awarded the Intermediate Certificate.

I very soon realised that my own experiences of divorce, bereavement and living with a depressive had all served to equip me to have empathy with others suffering in similar ways. The course was quite demanding, both from the point of view of studying and also from the self-analysing that we were required to do. Revealing my inmost thoughts and feelings to others in the group was not easy but produced a deal of healing from the pain I had experienced.

It was fifty-fifty theory and practical, and from time to time we undertook various assessments. The essays required were involved, and the course lecturer was very particular about the presentation of the essays, especially any quotes and references. We were required to read several books and discuss ways in which the various models and ways of counselling could be helpful or not so helpful. I found that some of the psychological models were difficult to accept as they were not in line with my Christian faith. I was able to defend my faith, and other people in the group would listen to me in the same way that I would listen to them. Towards the end of the course, some of them spoke to me about my faith and said that although they could not share the same faith, they admired and respected the stand that I took.

Another requirement of the course was that we should have personal counselling ourselves; I undertook this with a lady from Ascot. A particular revelation of my time with her was that of the loneliness of my childhood and also the repeating pattern of rejection coming through first my father and my sister Beryl, then at junior school and then through Keiran. Having met the requirement, I ceased this activity and concentrated my energies on the course, the homework and working at the counselling centre.

At the end of the two years, I gained the Certificate, but I decided not to continue in the third year to do the Diploma. This was mainly because I had a disagreement with the course tutor, who stated very plainly and unequivocally that an essential requirement of the Diploma course was one hundred percent attendance. My view was that this was virtually impossible to guarantee. For one thing, George needed to take his holiday during the winter months as the summer months were too busy in the garden for him to take time off. I also suggested that during the course of a whole year, it was impossible to predict whether at some point in time there would be a need for absence due to illness. The course tutor was adamant: without one hundred percent attendance there would be no Diploma. Bearing in mind George's history of illness, I thought it was very important for him to have his holiday, and if that holiday was in the winter then so be it. I could not expect him to forego his holidays for a whole year so that I could gain a Diploma when my future did not envisage paid counselling but rather volunteering – i.e. unpaid. So I declined to undertake this third year because I knew that with such inflexible criteria, there was no way I would get the Diploma at the end.

Funnily enough, George seemed to resent me volunteering for the centre; whether I chose an evening or a Saturday morning, any time I was there was wrong and took too much of my time for his liking. I have never managed to uncover why it was he was less than happy at my helping others – I think part of it was to do with the fact I was not being paid.

Eventually, I left my current role and changed over to working for another counselling service organised by the churches in a nearby town. This meant I could use a small room at the church, and I offered my services there usually during one morning a week when others were also in the building. Again, I was not paid but felt that it was a service I could give to others and, hopefully, at the same time, bring some Christian input into their lives. The drawback of this set-up at Woodside was that there were no proper supervision sessions like those I was used to. Consequently, it is possible to feel unsupported and lacking in checks and balances that provide a means of knowing you are on the right track. Supervision sessions enable an examination of the counselling session, giving another's insight into the problem(s) and ideas for moving the client forward. Thankfully, partly because my sessions did not interfere with George's plans and also because it was a service for the church, I gained more support for this venture.

Because of the secular emphasis of the training that I had undertaken, I decided to look for a Christian counselling course. I attended a three-month course at Southampton which gave me an insight into the Christian model of counselling. The course involved travelling to Southampton on a Friday afternoon, attending sessions on Friday evening and Saturday and then driving home again on the Saturday late afternoon. Accommodation overnight was provided by people who attended the church there, and I stayed with a delightful family. It would have been nice to have been able to undertake a more lengthy course at Waverley Abbey but this too was very expensive, and I could not justify spending such large sums of money when it was not my intention to charge for my services. Had I been twenty years younger, I could have viewed the cost as an investment which I would recoup with professional fees over the years, but at my age this was not my priority.

In the summer of 2006 I assembled material, then organised and ran a group, for divorcees. Looking back over the programme and the group, I have mixed feelings about my venture. To begin with, I compiled the material by researching several books on the subject and seeking the support of the organisation for whom I was working as a volunteer. Having gained approval for my material, I sought the backing of the church leadership to advertise the group among the local community. Sadly, I did not receive the help and support I expected but was told to inform the local churches; a public advertisement was not deemed to be appropriate. I tried to inform local churches and doctors' surgeries and managed to get a small slot on the local radio. The course ran in the church's coffee bar, which was a nice, informal-style room but unfortunately located next to the main church where on several occasions the music group was practising at the same time. This made the sessions harder to manage. However, there were sufficient numbers for the course to run, and all the participants came for the whole duration. I'm trusting God that he will have used that time to benefit them.

In later years I have been privileged to be a member of the pastoral team at Spring Harvest, and an elder at the church invited me to join his team. Initially, I was conscious of my lack of 'ministry' experience, but as time went on, I gradually became more confident in prayerfully listening to God as well as the person coming for help. Also, the counselling experience there is concentrated into a one-off one-hour session. Being in the prayerful environment of Spring Harvest is great; the team were friendly and we had a good rapport together. The team used to spend most of the day in their designated hut and we had a rota for being on duty and available to talk to people. The people coming to the team for help varied enormously, and as the days went by, gradually more and more people were coming to the team. It was a very rewarding few days – the only downside being the weather (springtime can be unpredictable).

Over the years, and in my experience, a lot of the people I have spent time with have been suffering from various forms of depression. It is a true saying that to understand and appreciate anyone's problem you need to "have worn the moccasins for three days". In other words, you need to be able to say, "I've got the T-shirt," as at least a starter, to be in a position to offer any real empathy. My experience of years living with George's depression day after day was now being put to good use.

"Praise be to the God and Father of our Lord Jesus Christ, the Father of compassion and the God of all comfort, who comforts us in all our troubles, so that we can comfort those in any trouble with the comfort we ourselves receive from God."[8]

---

[8] 2 Corinthians 1:3-4

CHAPTER SEVENTEEN

Woodside Church

OUR ADVENT INTO WOODSIDE CHURCH CAME AS A RESULT of changes in Bracknell. Following the 'Toronto Blessing'[9], there were many changes, some good and some, sadly, not so good. It was hard to leave a church that I had been part of since 1975. George and I had been married there and George baptised there. Our three girls also had been baptised there and effectively grown up and left home during our time there.

But we just couldn't stay and be a part of what was happening and so decided to move on. We looked for another church family to join locally without success and were becoming despondent when we finally went to visit Woodside to see what sort of a church it was. Woodside was a ten-mile drive away, but as we arrived and stepped through the entrance, we looked at each other and just knew that was where we were supposed to be. Woodside Church was a great blessing. The preaching was excellent and the worship a joy to be part of.

During the time we were part of the church there, I was able to be join the worship group for a while, and we were very encouraged by our house group that met weekly. I was given the privilege of leading the worship on occasion, and the first time was quite nerve-wracking; this was something new and I wanted to get it right. I prepared the songs, prayers and Bible reading beforehand, asking God to help me choose the right songs etc. But the enemy tries hard to knock us off track, and the night before the Sunday morning, George's mum had a

---

[9] A time of revival when the Holy Spirit was actively moving in many churches.

fall. She lived in sheltered housing and it was the Saturday evening. George had been to see her that day, as indeed he went most days to see that she was OK. That evening we were relaxing when he said he felt uneasy despite his earlier visit and wanted to go and check on her. When he entered her flat, he could hear a faint "Help!" and investigated. She had fallen fully clothed into the bath and could not get out. He called for an ambulance and she was taken into the hospital, and we both felt it was right that I should go with her. She was very confused and kept telling everyone, "I want the doctor!" When eventually we were seen by the duty doctor in A&E, she even repeatedly told him, "I want the doctor," to which he replied, "I *am* the doctor." Following this episode, she was in hospital for some time. The night in A&E was very long, and I arrived home the following morning having had no sleep and due to lead worship very shortly! How was I going to manage? I felt like a zombie walking. But God had it all in hand; it was an amazing experience that He filled me with calm and literally took over the whole thing. The service went ahead, and although I was the visible leader, really God was in charge and enabled that time. It reinforced to me the truth that, "My grace is sufficient for you, for my power is made perfect in weakness."[10]

Woodside was a large and active church, and George and I took on another new role in that together we led a house group for young adults. The group was great fun and, although we were of a slightly older generation, worked really well. Only recently we reminisced about the various members of the group and wondered what they are doing now. We know of the outcome of one particular young lady, Gemma, who was still single and desperate to find the right man for her. We prayed together about this, and not too long after she moved away. Imagine our delight when a year or so later she paid us a surprise visit and introduced her fiancé. Later still we learned she had had twins. So God certainly answered our prayers for Gemma more than we asked or imagined.

One of the activities I helped with was the Alpha course. Over the years four of my friends have come to the Alpha course with differing outcomes. First of all was Dick, the husband of one of my bridge-

---

[10]   2 Corinthians 12:9

playing circle. He had been diagnosed with stomach cancer and given a two-year prognosis. He came to Alpha and accepted Christ. As his illness progressed, I was able to visit him at home and his faith became a great comfort to him.

Second was another friend's husband who came along. He, however, was involved in the freemasons and didn't seem to be able to differentiate between the God the masons have as part of their rituals and the real Saviour. He was likeable and clever with a lovely family and good income. After the second or third session, he recognised the need for faith in Christ, but he evidently did not accept that it was relevant for him on a personal basis and sadly walked away. As I write this, he now has early onset dementia and it is sad that he turned away from Christ all those years ago.

Delia had been a long-standing friend from the days when I worked at social services. She was a widow, and I had several conversations with her about God. Sadly, she lost her husband very suddenly, and subsequently endured disappointment and difficulties. She found it hard to get past the loss of her husband and was angry with God for taking him away. Following her move into new accommodation, she had a comfortable life, and her daughter and grandchildren were a comfort to her. Delia agreed to come to Alpha, and I hoped that the clear presentation and the working of the Holy Spirit would convince her of the truth. Delia is an enigma; she has not to my knowledge made a commitment to Jesus but does come to church events and firmly supported our SENIORS group. I continue to pray one day she will have a revelation of God's love for her that will transform her reluctance to trust Him. Delia is such a lovely person, and I would love to know if she has finally taken that step of faith.

Daisy was another friend of mine from the bridge club. She and I were partners for a while; she was great fun and quite unpredictable sometimes, making outrageous bids when playing the game. Bridge players will know that sometimes risky bids can come off and produce an amazing score and at other times backfire and the opposite result ensues. She was a good friend, and we often talked about her granddaughter who, sadly, was anorexic. Her granddaughter had had various treatments and interventions but to no avail. Her condition was chronic and was so bad that it seriously threatened her health. I offered to pray for her granddaughter and she gladly accepted my offer. I tried to support her in her anxiety over the granddaughter's illness, and we shared a mixture of happy and sad times. One day I was talking to Daisy, and she spoke about how she would like her life to change. I asked her what she really, *really* wanted. To my surprise, she answered that she wanted a faith like mine! Alpha courses were a continual feature at Woodside Church and she agreed to come on one. We were all set for her to come along, but then at the last minute the course was cancelled because there were not enough participants. Following that, I made enquiries and managed to secure her a place on another Alpha course. This time she took a fall during a visit to the theatre and broke her hip. That event put her out of circulation for quite a while, but eventually she recovered. I looked again for another Alpha course and I discovered that another local church was running a group from a member's home which was literally just up the road from where Daisy lived. This was good, because although I would go with her to the first session to enable her to feel comfortable, I would then be able to back out and leave her to attend the other sessions on her own.

At the third time of trying, Daisy attended the Alpha course and got on well with the leaders. Following the Holy Spirit weekend away she spoke to me with her eyes bright and gleaming. She told me that she had made a commitment to Christ and that her long-standing fear of death had gone. Praise God – He did a marvellous work in Daisy! No wonder the enemy tried his best to prevent her from attending the course.

Just two weeks later Daisy died suddenly. Her husband had gone out to play golf and returned home to find she had had an embolism. How marvellous is God's timing! He knew Daisy's time was near and despite the enemy's efforts to deter her, He purposed to give her that opportunity of turning to Him in faith.

CHAPTER EIGHTEEN

West Hill Church – A New Challenge

OUR MOVE FROM WOODSIDE CHURCH WAS PRECEDED BY George sensing God saying that we should be attending a more local church. Admittedly, travelling to church was a journey of ten miles door to door, and attending on Sundays and mid-week house groups, plus sometimes coffee duty in the café, meant a lot of journeys.

So we looked for a church locally, beginning close to home, then expanding our search. The nearest church was a C of E just a few minutes' walk away, next to the senior school where Lizzie, Jane and May had had their secondary education. We tried going there for a few weeks but thought that it was not for us, so our next port of call was West Hill Church. It was a smaller church than we had been used to in Woodside and seemed quite old-fashioned, but the people were warm and welcoming. On our second visit the pastor told us that we were just what he had been praying for – a couple to lead a new group for the old people. We were aghast; we had never worked with old people before and did not feel we had any gifting in this regard. However, we agreed to think about it.

The current set-up was that they had a Bible study for the elderly ladies on a Monday afternoon and they wanted a more low-key general group to which non-church people could be invited. George and the pastor went to visit a community group at a church in a nearby town and came back with visions of how *not* to do the group. We decided to give it a try, and a small team of helpers joined us. The simple format would be coffee / tea / biscuit on arrival and a quiz on each table to encourage a talking point. After the answers to the quiz, people could split into groups for different activities – rummikub, scrabble, card games, painting, craft or jigsaw puzzles.

A soup and roll lunch would be served, together with cake and a cold drink. Once people had eaten but were still sitting together, one of the team would present a 'thought for the day' before people went home.

This simple format seemed to work well from the off, and we soon had a viable group of about twenty-four people, of whom about half were non-church-attenders. We ended up running this group for about six years, and over that time we praise God that several of those folk came to trust Christ as their saviour. John came to the Lord just before he died of cancer. He and his wife used to come to the group together; she was a champion rummikub player. They were a quiet couple but fun once you got to know them. Sadly, one day John found he was not able to get out of his chair and thus began a long investigation as to the reason for this. After extensive tests it was found that he had cancer and it was too advanced to be able to do much in the way of treatment. His wife nursed him at home, and during one of our visits, our pastor was able to lead him to Christ.

Patrick lived on his own. He had a son who lived in Australia and so received limited family support. He did have a good friend with whom he was able to do some activities, and at one time he was able to invite his friend to join us on one of our outings. Patrick was a tailor by trade and in years past had made suits for Fifty Shilling Tailors. He was also an artist and stamp collector. This gave us much in common, as I also dabble with painting and George is an avid stamp collector. Over time he told us how he had responded years ago to Billy Graham's appeal, but that was all. I couldn't help thinking of the parable of the sower who sowed seed on rocky ground, and I like to think that the regular biblical input and conversations we had with Patrick helped to soften that ground. Patrick lived alone in a flat near the town centre and one day had a fall. The next thing we knew was that he was in hospital and apparently had got sepsis. He managed to recover from this and, on his return to the group, gave a testimony of how God had been with him throughout his hospitalisation. It was great to hear his testimony and know that Patrick now had a personal and active faith in Christ.

Peggy was profoundly deaf. She used hearing aids, but I would always make sure that I spoke directly to her face as I knew she relied a lot on lip-reading. Peggy was an avid reader and used to have many books from the travelling library each visit. She was great fun and, again, a rummikub champion. There was a good deal of rivalry among the rummikub contingent and good-hearted competition. One day Peggy told me that she wanted to accept Christ, and I was able to lead her in a prayer. She was already a person who had a great sense of humour and enjoyed life despite her disabilities, and yet following her commitment, she showed a new level of joy. As I write this, I learned recently that Peggy has gone to be with Christ; I thank God for the privilege of getting to know her through our group.

Betty came to our group; she had been a churchgoer at a different church but never really felt accepted or part of things. We had some good conversations, and one day I challenged her about her personal faith and whether going to church was just a habit. She said she had found a new level of friendship and acceptance by coming to our group and was also happy to be coming to church as well. We prayed together, and she accepted Christ and, as far as I know, continues to be part of the church and group to this day.

Three others have moved on significantly in being open to the gospel and happily coming to church services, although I do not have any current knowledge of their walk with God. Some people see their walk with God as a very private thing and it is quite difficult to encourage them to be more open.

We had a lot of fun in the group and also devising the quiz sessions. George was a natural, and his humour and easy-going style soon enabled people to feel at ease. My job was to shop and cook the home-made soup, bearing in mind of course various people's allergies and likes/dislikes. Our soup had to be gluten-free, sugar-free and dairy-free – no mean task! The local council officials came to my home to inspect my kitchen and issue the necessary permit. They instructed me to adopt lengthy procedures and recording, all designed, I'm sure, with health and safety in mind, but rather over-the-top for a small contributor like me. One of the things I was supposed to do was to train my staff. *Staff* – what staff? I had no staff; I was it! 'Using a sledgehammer to crack a nut' comes to mind... Our helpers came to serve coffee and help wash up and generally chat to people. It was fun and a friendly atmosphere.

Each year I organised a summer outing in the month of August when our meetings took a break. At Christmas we usually went out to a local restaurant for lunch, and also the children from the pre-school group who met in the other church hall came to sing for us. The little tots singing their Christmas songs was so touching, and singing carols was also a firm favourite.

Moving house meant leaving the group behind, but we are still in touch with many of them and they came to visit us in our new home. We were pleased to welcome them and had a small 'garden party' in our garden with strawberries and a cream tea. Sadly, Covid-19 put a stop to that sort of activity, but we hope to be able to repeat the visit sometime in the future.

CHAPTER NINETEEN

Those Around Me

IT WOULD NOT BE GOOD TO END THIS ACCOUNT OF MY life without a chapter on the family and their achievements. You will remember our new family following my divorce and remarriage included three girls plus my father. The girls all did well at school: Lizzie went on to be a senior physiotherapist and unit manager; Jane a secondary school science teacher in Germany; and May a children's nurse and now an assoc. professor managing nursing courses. They are all happily married; the two older girls have celebrated their silver wedding anniversaries.

We have five grandchildren, all of whom are a joy and growing into adulthood. It has been a great source of pleasure and pride to see them growing up and to be involved in their childhood years. I have some lovely memories of all the things we were able to do with the children – all the usual things like going to the park, going to the fair and theme parks, going swimming and, while they were small, squeezing through the various tubes and tunnels etc. at the local indoor play area. I cherish the memories of school nativities, school concerts and other usual activities that have all been part of their growing up. Occasional visits to the cinema and pantomime and birthdays and Christmases all bring a smile. I must confess to being an embarrassment at a panto once when I was slow on the uptake of one of the jokes. I exploded with laughter about two or three minutes after everybody else and made a spectacle of myself.

My father who lived with us unfortunately continued in his characteristic ways and sadly conspired with my older sister to cut me out of his will. He lived with us for about five years, during which time I did everything for him and provided him with a comfortable home in his old age. At the time, my sister refused to make any contribution to caring for him and flatly refused even short visits, let alone a stay of a week or so to enable us to have a holiday. Nevertheless his continued rejection culminated in his conspiring with her behind my back. It was only because one of the girls was home from school and studying upstairs that we found out what was going on. George was very rightly incensed that we had offered him a home and his response was a slap in the face. We found a local residential home for him within a reasonable distance, and he moved there. We still visited him and offered him our support. He died about a year later at the age of eighty-nine. The relationship with my sister had never been great, and from the time when I was a child and "always in the way" she and I were not close. The episode with Dad did not help matters, but I tried to keep in touch and rang her from time to time, seeking to keep the relationship open. I think she probably had a guilty conscience because she was very reluctant to engage with me. However, I kept trying and eventually we did meet up on a few occasions for lunch out in Henley on Thames. Finally, however, even these visits fizzled out, and we were back to me making phone calls, our contact gradually becoming less and less as she never returned my calls. We did not hear from her for some time; then at Christmas we received a Christmas card from Australia! She had gone to live there near her two sons who had emigrated some years before. She didn't tell me she was going and never even said goodbye. It is sad to realise that there are some people that, no matter how hard you try, never really want you near them either physically or emotionally.

Going back to my girls, I am immensely proud of them and their achievements, both in their careers and home-making. They have each had their own challenges to overcome but they have come through with flying colours. I could say a lot more but that is their story to tell and not mine. All through the years they have been in my prayers, and I have seen God answering prayers for them and upholding them in difficult circumstances. I know they pray for me, and Lizzie and Jane are now an example to me, exercising their faith in God.

And what happened to George? He continued his work as a self-employed gardener until his retirement. He also developed quite a following among gardening societies, who used to invite him to do talks on every conceivable topic associated with gardening. I contributed to his lecture programme by making PowerPoint presentations on the laptop, and over the years he developed over forty lecture topics, all about plants, gardens and gardening. One comment from a local gardening club on their website said, "George can talk about anything, even knitting patterns!"

God opened a door for him to do some lectures on cruise ships, and as a result, we had several voyages to tropical and sub-tropical countries. Unfortunately, I have always suffered from seasickness, and some of his trips on smaller vessels were not an option for me. One notable trip through the Bay of Biscay in a force eleven gale resulted in my having to abandon ship and return home. The shipping company were fantastic in arranging my return to the U.K., but ever since, I have always measured my desire to travel against the possible results. The journeys and holidays we have had over the years have resulted in meeting a new group of good friends with whom we continue to be in contact. Travelling can produce transient memories of different places, but the friends we have made continue and are far more valuable than a few photos and videos.

Over the years George's speciality knowledge of tropical plants has developed and he is now writing his own book on tropical plants. The only problem is that he is so enthusiastic about his own garden that he has little time to spend in writing, so I've no idea if his book will ever be finished. Having told you about his lengthy battle with depression, it is with some admiration that I can now say that he is an example to me for being positive, especially during the long Covid-ridden months. Like me, he has turned seventy, and, after many years of hard physical work gardening, badly needs a knee replacement, but complications have meant this operation is on hold. Coupled together with the current situation with Covid-19, it seems unlikely his surgery will happen any time soon, if at all. But despite being in constant pain, he is cheerful and still manages to tend his beloved plants and raise money for charities.

As for me, getting older has meant some restrictions in some ways and compensating activities in others. The eczema from my youth has abated to easily manageable levels but has been replaced with asthma. This means restrictions on some physical activities and, sadly, has severely affected my voice and singing which I loved. There are other compensations though; I can still sew and read and dabble a bit at my other hobby of painting. I enjoy baking, and George's waistline unfortunately is a testimony to that, but I would never go so far as to say I can do anything more than basic home cooking.

Chapter Twenty

Moving On

IN 2017 WE MOVED TO A VILLAGE IN BUCKINGHAMSHIRE. Like most moves it was not without its 'moments', and it provides a story all of its own.

Once our three girls left home, we were not sure whether they would be coming back to live at home again. However, freedom is not easily given up, and none of them came home permanently again. So we had a four-bedroom house and only two of us living in it. This was a far cry from when we had moved in with three girls, my father, plus a dog and a cat!

We tried several times to move house, and I kept praying and asking God to show us where He wanted us to be. House-hunting was an eye-opener, and we spent many hours looking for a suitable place. We did find one that mostly fitted the bill, but the chain broke down and the whole thing collapsed. Time had been passing and several years had gone by. I was still praying but eventually got to the point of telling God, "If you don't want us to move, then OK, I will be content to stay here."

It was only after that things began to happen. We met a couple of workmen who were doing some remedial work for the church, and they advised us to contact a certain estate agent and put our house on the market on February 1st. We took their advice and got a buyer on that first day. We then went looking for a place to suit us but again looked endlessly at numerous places, none of which seemed suitable. Either they were bordering a motorway, or too expensive, or too small, or too dark. George was very fussy about having a south-facing garden so he could continue his passion for plants. One interesting property we saw was in Warborough, just off the main road from

Henley to Oxford. We went to look at a property, and on arriving, it was obvious that it was not for us as the garden was full of very large trees, so George dismissed it out of hand. However, across the road in the small close was another bungalow for sale with a different estate agent. We had a look around the outside and were being generally nosy when a local resident who was out in the garden spotted us. She had lived there many years, and chatting to her, it transpired that it was the bungalow where my sister used to live! I had only been invited to her home on one or two occasions many, many years ago. It seemed strange to be looking at what used to be her place with a view to buying it. However, the location was too far from the family and we did not pursue it.

We finally chose a place not far from where Lizzie was living, and the place seemed ideal for us with the exception of possibly an overly large rear garden. Our offer was accepted and things went ahead. During the lengthy legal process, we went on a long-arranged holiday in Florida with the family and grandchildren, and thanks to modern technology, a lot of the paperwork and instructions could be completed online.

My chest does not react well to the common cold, and unfortunately, I picked up a virus in Florida and was so ill that the airline would not allow me on the plane for the flight home. George and I stayed behind, and I was told to obtain a certificate to enable me to fly. That night I was taken into Miami Hospital and was there for several days whilst they treated my chest infection / pneumonia. George was able to stay in the hospital with me although he had to obtain a brand-new security pass each and every day due to their high levels of security there. It was amusing to have a recurrence of our 'water' episode in New York many years ago... I was told to drink a lot, so George would frequently go down the corridor to the water fountain to fetch me glasses of water. At the nurses' station they would remark to him frequently, "Are you wan-t-ing wa-t-er," joking with him about our English pronunciation of the word. Eventually, I was allowed to leave on condition I had an appointment with my doctor immediately on arriving home. We went to the airport and were told all the flights were full. We remained there, and I prayed for God to intervene and enable us to get on a flight home. He heard my prayer, and shortly afterwards two vacant seats appeared from nowhere and we were able to get on a plane home. I am now a firm advocate of holiday insurance, as we found out that my short stay for a few days in an American hospital cost $42,000.

The move was nearing completion; imagine our consternation to be gazumped! We had to start looking all over again, and the people buying our house had a deadline to move in due to the fact they were getting married the week after the set moving date.

So we looked at a small village in Buckinghamshire and agreed the little bungalow was suitable for us. The garden certainly pleased George, which was the main thing. There was a lot of work to be done on the property, but we decided to go ahead. And so we moved in May, four years ago, and immediately joined the local Baptist church there. Once the decision had been taken, we moved in the space of six weeks, which was a miracle in itself as solicitors often take around twelve weeks or even longer to complete. The people buying our old house moved in on time and were able to have their wedding as planned.

It has taken us a couple of years to renovate the bungalow, but the place is now largely repaired and the garden transformed. Now we look forward to finding out what the Lord has for us here. George is already somewhat of a local institution now, being involved in all sorts of gardening projects in the village. Currently, we are living with strict Covid-19 restrictions, needing to take extra care because of age and asthma, and a lot of our church activities are curtailed. But this too shall pass, and there will be something for us to be part of... Will God speak through a small voice, a Bible reading, through others in our house group, friends, family, other people or circumstances? If I've learned nothing else in writing this book, I have seen how God has led me over the years.

Sadly, as I come to the end of this account of my life, I have just learned of the death of my very dear friend of over fifty years, Mary. She and her husband were a great support to me over the years, and I am so thankful for her life and friendship. She came to know Jesus in later years, and I feel comforted that I know she is now with him. Also, in the last few weeks my next-door neighbour and friend suddenly died within a very few weeks of being diagnosed with cancer.

I had shared my faith with her and she had always responded by recounting the sad events in her life that she blamed God for. So I was very upset when she died, because despite my sharing with her, she had always refused to believe. Because of Covid, I was not allowed to visit, as only carers and the family were allowed to see her. In the final days of her life, I sent a brief note which her daughter read to her, again reminding her of the reason Jesus came so that we could be forgiven; then, having done all I could, I had to leave it with the Lord. I am not given to dreams and it has never happened before, but following her death, I did experience a dream in which she appeared to me and was alive. "Oh, I'm so glad you're alive after all," I said, but that was the end of my dream. I have pondered this and wonder whether that was simply my wishful thinking or whether it was God comforting me with the knowledge that she was with Him.

Reminding myself of what God has done not only makes me thankful but gives me confidence that He is still on the throne even in these days of lockdown and Covid-19. As I write this, we at last have hope of coming through this pandemic and I have had two vaccinations which will allow me to move about more freely. Normal life has not resumed yet, but there is light at the end of the tunnel.

Looking back over my life and writing this book has been a revelation to me. I'm finally coming to a place of acceptance and thankfulness – thankfulness for all the good things God has done in my life, how He has brought good things out of bad, and a knowledge that He really is with me whether or not I feel him near. "So do not fear, for I am with you; do not be dismayed, for I am your God. I will strengthen you and help you; I will uphold you with my righteous right hand."[11]

In the Old Testament we read about memorials made of piles of stones. These were so that the people would remember what God had done. They would act as a reminder, and the people were to tell their children so that they would also remember. This retelling of my life story also has that same purpose to some extent – remembering and appreciating what God has done, giving Him the praise and thanks and proclaiming to any who will read this God's faithfulness and

---

[11] Isaiah 41:10

power. I remember where God has brought me from, and it's not of my own doing but of His. "For it is by grace you have been saved, through faith – and this is not from yourselves, it is the gift of God – not by works, so that no one can boast. For we are God's handiwork, created in Christ Jesus to do good works, which God prepared in advance for us to do."[12]

I don't know where I would be today if it wasn't for His faithfulness and mercy, forgiving me over and over again. I have a piece of cross-stitch sewing like a sampler which I made and framed and hung on the wall many years ago. The words on the sampler say "Grow in the Grace of our Lord Jesus Christ". It's only now that I am coming to really appreciate that grace and, like the song says, it's truly amazing.

The rejection from my father, sister and first husband reinforced in me the idea that I was not good enough, but over the years I have come to understand my value as a child of God. Learning about God's grace and knowing in my heart as well as my head that God loves me has brought freedom from trying to be somebody I'm not. When I think of what the world values, I am nothing by comparison. I have no degree, no career, no status, no special talent or skill, nothing that the world admires. Yet God has blessed me so much with a beautiful and lovely family, He has blessed me with lasting friendships and His provision for all my needs.

When I recall my childhood song 'Jesus bids us shine', truly my light has been small and sometimes very dim, but He has kept my light burning and given me opportunities to shine for Him in my small corner.

God bless you.

---

[12] Ephesians 2:8-10

Similar Books from the Publisher

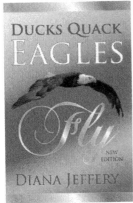

Ducks Quack, Eagles Fly
Diana Jeffery
ISBN 978-1-907509-30-8

Mother of six children, primary school teacher and public speaker, Diana has faced many challenges in her life. She lost her first child and was told she could not expect to have more children; she was recommended to abort her second child; she faced the financial challenges of raising six children on her husband's teaching wage; she faced life-threatening diseases; finally, she and her husband were forced out of their teaching jobs by malicious false allegations. But being a Christian means that life is for overcoming, not complaining. Her ordinary yet extraordinary tale of Christian family life is an encouragement for all Christian mothers.

Mary Something-Else
Mary Hughes
ISBN 978-1-907509-92-6

"I want something else!" demanded two-year-old Mary. "Well, what do you want?" her mother asked. "A sweet?" "Yes," she replied, grabbing the opportunity, "but I want something else!" "How about a cuddle?" "Yes... but I want something else." Mary's journey would take her to Africa and back, meeting many interesting people, looking for the 'something else' that would change her life forever...

Books available from all good bookshops
or from the publisher:

www.onwardsandupwards.org/shop